RED ZONE

CUBA AND THE BATTLE AGAINST EBOLA IN WEST AFRICA

D1553280

To Fidel, on his ninetieth birthday.

RED ZONE

CUBA AND THE BATTLE AGAINST EBOLA IN WEST AFRICA

Enrique Ubieta Gómez

Pathfinder

NEW YORK   LONDON   MONTREAL   SYDNEY

Edited by Martín Koppel and Mary-Alice Waters

Translated from the Spanish by Catriona Goss

Copyright © 2019 by Pathfinder Press
Copyright © 2016 by Enrique Ubieta Gómez and Casa Editora Abril
All rights reserved

ISBN 978-1-60488-114-1
Library of Congress Control Number 2019955382
Manufactured in the United States of America

First edition, 2019
Second printing, 2020

COVER DESIGN: Toni Gorton

COVER PHOTOS: From top to bottom: (1) Cuban medical volunteers
unload supplies on arrival in Freetown, Sierra Leone, to join
fight against Ebola epidemic, October 2014. (2) Cuban physicians
treating patients, Coyah, Guinea, January 2015 (*Enrique Ubieta*).
(3) Doctors in protective suits with patients about to be released
from Coyah treatment unit, January 2015 (*Cuban Medical Brigade
in Guinea/Facebook page*). (4) Cuban volunteers with recovered
patients, Coyah, January 2015 (*Enrique Ubieta*).

Pathfinder
www.pathfinderpress.com
E-mail: pathfinder@pathfinderpress.com

"When I was talking with the students today, I told them we need fifty volunteer doctors to go to Algeria. . . .

"We're certain there won't be any lack of volunteers. Just fifty. We're sure more will volunteer, as an expression of our people's spirit of solidarity with a fraternal people who are worse off than we are. Worse off than we are!

"Today we can send fifty; in eight or ten years we don't know how many, but we know we'll be able to help sister countries, because with each passing year we'll have more doctors. Every passing year, more students will enter medical school."

Fidel Castro
Opening of "Victory of Playa
Girón" School of Medicine
Havana, October 1962

CONTENTS

Maps

PHOTO SECTIONS FOLLOW PAGES 82, 146

OTHER PHOTOS

Enrique Ubieta (second from right) together with Liberian health minister Bernice Dahn and two Cuban TV reporters, Tomás Oliveros (left) and Yordanis Rodríguez. Ubieta, Oliveros, and Rodríguez accompanied Cuban medical teams in West Africa for several weeks in early 2015.

ABOUT THE AUTHOR

Enrique Ubieta Gómez is the editor of *Cuba Socialista*, theoretical magazine of the Central Committee of Cuba's Communist Party. He was also editor of *La Calle del Medio*, a monthly magazine of cultural debate, from 2008 to 2017. He is a member of the National Union of Writers and Artists of Cuba (UNEAC). Born in Havana in 1958, Ubieta was managing editor of the student newspaper *Chispa* at the Lenin Vocational High School. He joined the Union of Young Communists in 1975. After graduating in 1983 from the University of Kiev, Ukraine, he taught philosophy at the José Martí Teachers Institute in Camagüey, Cuba. From 1994 to 1999 he was director of the Center for the Study of José Martí. Ubieta has been a member of the Communist Party of Cuba since 1986. He has received numerous awards and distinctions.

From April 1999 to March 2000, he visited some of the most remote areas of Nicaragua, Honduras, Guatemala, and Haiti, reporting on the work of Cuban volunteer doctors and nurses who provided medical care after the devastation of Hurricane Mitch. From that experience he wrote the 2002 book *La utopía rearmada: Historias de un viaje*

al Nuevo Mundo (Utopia rearmed: Report on a trip to the New World).

From June 2005 to March 2006 he traveled throughout Venezuela to report on the efforts—which involved thousands of Cuban medical volunteers—to expand health care to workers and peasants in Venezuela in what became known as Mission *Barrio Adentro* (Into the neighborhood). Drawing on that trip he wrote *Venezuela rebelde: Solidaridad vs. dinero* (Rebellious Venezuela: Solidarity vs. money).

PREFACE

Róger Calero and Mary-Alice Waters

Red Zone: Cuba and the Battle Against Ebola in West Africa is not a book about doctors, epidemics, or medical care, as central as those topics are to the remarkable account you are about to read. First and foremost, the book is "about the solidarity and internationalism that are at the heart of the Cuban Revolution," as author Enrique Ubieta told the audience at its launching in Havana in February 2016.

In August and September 2014, the World Health Organization and the governments of three West African countries, Liberia, Sierra Leone, and Guinea, issued international calls for help in combating the largest epidemic on record of the deadly Ebola virus. In contrast to the meager and callously self-serving response of capitalist powers, especially the United States, France, and the United Kingdom, Cuba's revolutionary socialist government acted rapidly.

Within three days of a call to Cuban president Raúl Castro from Ban Ki-moon, secretary-general of the United Nations, more than 12,000 Cuban medical professionals had volunteered, many with experience responding to epidemics and disasters from Haiti to Pakistan to Central America. Of those volunteers, 256 Cuban doctors, nurses, and health care technicians were selected and trained for the mission.

Eight months later, when the last member of the Cuban medical brigade returned home in May 2015, the Ebola epidemic in West Africa had been virtually eradicated.

Ubieta's firsthand reporting of this fight, told largely through accounts by the Cuban participants themselves, paints a graphic picture of the social disaster that unfolded in these three countries in 2014 and 2015, and how the enemy was defeated.

The volunteers were given intensive training in handling the highly lethal Ebola virus at Cuba's world-famous Pedro Kourí Institute of Tropical Medicine. The first teams were on their way to the crisis areas in a matter of weeks.

The small island nation of Cuba provided what was most needed and what no other country even tried to deliver: hundreds of doctors, nurses, technicians, and public health specialists *on the ground, caring for thousands of desperately ill human beings and their families and communities traumatized by the killer disease.*

For the Cuban people and their communist leadership, such a response was nothing new. It was simply one more example of the political course that began with the January 1959 triumph of a revolution that brought to power a government representing working people. A government of, by, and for the humble, as they often describe it. That course— at home and abroad—is one of solidarity, not charity. From Asia and Africa, to Latin America and the Caribbean, they have shared in the hardships and struggles of others seeking national sovereignty and independence.

To give but one example, in the very first years of the revolutionary transformation of Cuba, the new government sent not only weapons but also doctors to aid the embattled National Liberation Front of Algeria fighting for independence from France. And on the ships returning to the island, Cubans brought war orphans and wounded combatants for medical care and education.

Sending doctors to Algeria in the early 1960s "was like a beggar offering his help," said Cuba's then Minister of Public Health José Ramón Machado Ventura some thirty years later. "But we knew the Algerian people needed it even more than we did and that they deserved it." No words better capture the internationalism of the Cuban Revolution.

∿

This unmatched record explains why the presentation of the Cuban edition of *Zona Roja* at the 2016 Havana International Book Fair was a high point of that annual event. Among those in the standing-room-only crowd were two dozen members of the volunteer Cuban contingent that waged this fight. The atmosphere in the room was filled with camaraderie among the doctors and nurses who had answered the call for help. Their sense of collective pride at having taken part in this battle—and, for the rest of us present, the respect and admiration for these internationalist volunteers—was palpable.

The heads of the Cuban medical brigades in Sierra Leone, Guinea, and Liberia each spoke, along with the author and Abel Prieto, former longtime Cuban minister of culture and now head of the Office of the José Martí Program in Havana. Prieto saluted "the selflessness, principles, and convictions" of the Cuban volunteers, saying that "they exemplify the purest ideals of the Cuban Revolution."

He reminded participants of the words of Fidel Castro, historic leader of the Cuban Revolution, at the opening of the Ebola mission in October 2014: "The medical personnel who will go anywhere to save lives, even at risk of losing their own, are the greatest example of solidarity a human being can offer, above all because they aren't motivated by material interest."

The discipline, courage, sense of humor, and joy of these Cuban volunteers comes through time and again in these pages. The political course and moral values their actions embody are an expression of the social relations only a truly socialist revolution can produce. They register the economic, social, and political conquests working people in Cuba have made since they freed their country from US imperialist domination and took power out of the hands of domestic and foreign capitalists and plantation landowners.

Many have asked, "Why did no other country in the world respond to the Ebola epidemic the way Cuba did? Can't Cuba's medical system and internationalist missions be emulated by other countries?" The answer is no secret. Cuba's proletarian internationalism is the product of a socialist revolution. It cannot be grafted onto other nations, nor reproduced by men and women who have not been transformed by a similar revolutionary class struggle.

∼

The first edition of *Zona Roja* was published by Casa Editora Abril, the publishing house of Cuba's Union of Young Communists.

These new editions—*Red Zone* in English, *Zona Roja* in Spanish—join the arsenal of Pathfinder books and pamphlets that tell the truth about the Cuban Revolution to new generations of workers, farmers, and youth in the United States and worldwide. These titles offer political lessons to study and examples to emulate for working people and youth everywhere. For those fighting for health, safety, and dignity on the job. Against imperialism's bloody and never-ending wars and assaults on national sovereignty. For an end to the discrimination and brutalities faced daily by African Americans, women, immigrants, and other oppressed layers. Against debt slavery, farm foreclosures, and capitalism's destruction of our natural environment. And all the other ravages of capitalist property relations.

The record the Cuban internationalists recount here helps us understand what a socialist revolution is. Eradicating exploitation changes not only the circumstances in which we live and work. It begins to change what capitalism teaches us is "immutable" human nature. Cuba's example points us to the only class forces that can and will make it possible for working people to fundamentally transform ourselves as we transform social conditions.

~

Red Zone also provides a compelling refutation of the US government's slanders against Cuba's internationalist medical cooperation.

Precisely because the example of this cooperation is so powerful and so welcomed by working people around the world, Washington has intensified efforts to peddle the lie that Cuban doctors, nurses, and medical technicians who volunteer for these missions are victims of "exploitative and coercive labor practices," "human trafficking," even "modern slavery!" The US rulers aim in particular to entice Cuban doctors with the siren song of the princely incomes that most physicians in the United States and other capitalist countries have been taught to expect as "fair" remuneration for the embossed piece of paper on their office walls.

Washington's slanderous campaign is simply another front in the six-decade-long economic war by US Democratic and Republican administrations alike aimed at isolating and economically strangling the Cuban people. These measures, once again tightened since 2017, have the objective of ultimately restoring control of Cuba's land, labor, factories, and natural resources to capitalist hands, from which they were ripped by working people in the opening years of the revolution.

There is no better answer to the US government's efforts to tarnish the Cuban Revolution's medical internationalism than the response of thousands in 2014 to the request for aid in the fight against Ebola. When members of the brigade were on the ground, millions in Cuba closely followed the news of what was happening there. Despite concerns for the volunteers and the risks of introducing the disease into Cuba, the example set by the volunteers in West Africa was deeply popular on the island.

Cuba's system of primary health care and medical treatment, at no cost to individuals and their families, is a conquest of the revolution that the Cuban people justly take pride in. It's not a commodity bought and sold for profit. It starts from saving lives, from the right of every person to health care, and from basic human solidarity at home and abroad.

In addition to the victory in the battle against Ebola, readers will learn in *Red Zone* how Cuban medical brigades helped combat a deadly cholera epidemic in Haiti in 2010. How such internationalist missions have provided desperately needed medical and other disaster relief in countries across Central and South America and the Caribbean to Pakistan, the Pacific islands, and beyond. How Cuban medical personnel were already at work in thirty-two African countries when the Ebola epidemic erupted.

The exemplary conduct of the Cuban volunteers won the admiration of other medical personnel with whom they shared the trenches, both health workers from the three West African countries and those from elsewhere around the globe. Ubieta also describes the process, sometimes more winding than others, through which the volunteers won the trust of patients and their families, many of whom ended up asking for themselves or loved ones to be treated by Cuban doctors and nurses.

The Cuban volunteers maintained the most rigorous safety procedures, especially in the "red zone"—the area of treatment centers with the highest contamination levels, where patients were quarantined. Only one Cuban contracted the disease; he recovered and returned to the front lines of the battle two months later.

Despite the "space suits" and other necessary safety measures, the Cubans treated the patients and their family members as fellow human beings, not a biohazard. They fought for the life of every patient, even when doing so wasn't "cost-effective," since the person seemed to have little chance of survival. If a patient was going to die, they would die with dignity, the Cuban doctors and nurses insisted. And their families would know that everything possible had been done to cure them.

The volunteers took an interest in the patients, asking about their work and their families. They called patients by their names, not by a bed number. In the often over-crowded treatment centers, they never asked a patient lying on the floor to stand up to be examined. These were the social attitudes the patients came to recognize in the Cuban doctors and nurses, even when they were sealed in their "astronaut"-like bodysuits and masks.

∽

The Cuban volunteers in West Africa were part of the Henry Reeve International Contingent, launched in September 2005. President Fidel Castro initiated the contingent that year in response to Hurricane Katrina. The hope was they would be allowed to provide assistance to residents of New Orleans and the surrounding Louisiana bayous devastated by the storm.

The US government, however, flatly rejected Cuba's offer to send 1,500 medical personnel to help. Instead, Washington brutally left working people there to fend for themselves, knowing full well that medical attention, food, and water were woefully lacking.

This contempt for working people's lives and welfare on the part of the wealthy US capitalist families—and of the government and twin political parties through which they exercise their exploitation and class rule—has been repeated many times over, both before and after Katrina. In the past few years alone, we've seen the social catastrophe in the wake of Hurricane Maria in Puerto Rico in 2017; the devastation in Florida and the Carolinas in 2019; and countless floods, wildfires, and other disasters in Texas, California, and across the United States. *And around the world.*

While many such occurrences are natural in origin, the catastrophic *social consequences* for tens and hundreds of millions are a product of capitalism.

As this book goes to press in late 2019, a new outbreak of Ebola in the Congo, second only in scope to the West Africa epidemic, has passed its one-year mark and still threatens to spread. Once again, the response by the profiteers' governments and "charitable" institutions hasn't gone much beyond declarations of "a public health emergency of international concern." Meanwhile, the capitalist owners of giant US and other multinational pharmaceutical corporations compete for market share for their new Ebola vaccines and treatments.

Cuba's "army of white coats," as Fidel Castro aptly called them in 2014, acts in stark contrast to capitalist "medicine." Serving in 64 countries, these volunteers often work and live in the most remote rural regions or worst-off urban working-class neighborhoods. These are areas that profit-maximizing hospitals and "health-care" conglomerates stay as far away from as possible. As do most physicians who graduate from medical school in the capitalist world, convinced that their diplomas entitle them to big bucks and the best comforts their class privilege can offer.

The goal of Cuba's internationalist cooperation is not simply to provide needed medical personnel where none currently exist. The Cuban government strives to contribute to building a medical infrastructure in these countries wherever possible, helping establish medical schools in some countries, bringing students to Cuba for medical training at little or no cost, and assisting in developing networks of primary care clinics.

Cuba's revolutionary government has extended medical assistance to countries with which it doesn't have diplomatic relations as well. That was the case, for example, when 2,400 doctors, nurses, and others went to the mountainous Kashmir region of Pakistan in 2005 following the 7.6 magnitude earthquake that killed some 80,000 human beings there. Cuban medical volunteers set up 30 field hospitals, later donated to the Pakistan government. Cuba provided 1,000 scholarships to students in the region to study at the Latin American School of Medicine in Havana.

Like other missions abroad, the fight against Ebola was a learning experience for the Cuban medical personnel involved. This was especially true for younger brigade members, who have never themselves (nor, as years go by, their parents or even grandparents) lived or worked under the dog-eat-dog social relations bred by capitalist exploitation and rendered even more brutal by imperialist oppression.

In *Red Zone*, Ubieta said at the 2016 launching, "I write about the seeds we are sowing inside and outside of ourselves. Every time a Cuban doctor takes part in a mission abroad, they renew themselves as revolutionaries."

Some people contend "that the epic moments of the Cuban Revolution are a thing of the past," Ubieta noted, and "that Cubans should concern themselves only with their own individual, everyday problems, which can sometimes be overwhelming.

"And then suddenly you hear the battle cry, like the request we received for aid. And thousands turn out, volunteering to go. Solidarity is very much alive in the Cuban people."

December 7, 2019

"Some say we should concern ourselves only with our own everyday problems. But every time a Cuban doctor takes part in a mission like the one in West Africa, they renew themselves as revolutionaries."
— Enrique Ubieta, February 2016

February 2016 launch of Cuban edition of *Zona Roja* (Red Zone) at Havana International Book Fair.

Top: Panel presenting book. From left, Doctors Juan Carlos Dupuy, Carlos Castro, and Jorge Delgado; Enrique Ubieta, book's author; Abel Prieto, former minister of culture; Javier Dueñas, director of Casa Editora Abril, which published first edition in Spanish. Dupuy, Castro, and Delgado headed Cuban medical brigades in Liberia, Guinea, and Sierra Leone during fight against Ebola.

Bottom: Audience at book launch included numerous doctors and nurses who were part of volunteer mission in West Africa. In front row, left, Maité Rivero, who as Cuba's ambassador to Guinea worked closely with medical brigade.

PREAMBLE

Enrique Ubieta Gómez

In 1959 there were 6,286 doctors in Cuba, and roughly 3,000 abruptly emigrated, lured by tempting job prospects offered by the US government. That was one of the many ways Washington tried to undermine the economic and social foundations of the newly victorious Cuban Revolution. Despite the small number of doctors who remained, however, Cuba's first long-term internationalist medical brigade went to Algeria in 1963.

Today Cuba has more than 85,000 doctors—7.7 per 1,000 inhabitants, the highest ratio in the world. The 2014–2015 battle against Ebola in West Africa was a brief but heroic episode in the revolution's long tradition of solidarity. The widespread media coverage Cuba's role received made it seem like something unusual. So too did the real danger to which the participants in this battle were exposed: a highly contagious and lethal filovirus about which little was or is known. Another factor was the international political context, marked by the opening of the process of reestablishing diplomatic relations between the Cuban and US governments.

In reality, however, sending 256 doctors and nurses to the West African countries struck by the Ebola epidemic continued a tradition spanning more than five decades.

I had the privilege of writing about two previous internationalist experiences. In 1999–2000, after Hurricanes Mitch and George, I accompanied Cuban medical brigade members to three Central American and one Caribbean country—Nicaragua, Honduras, Guatemala, and Haiti. It was a time when many had shamefully abandoned professed ideals of social justice. While revolutionary perspectives were in need of new interpretations, the poor, the humble—or the fragile, as Pope Francis would call them on his 2015 visit to Havana—continued to await justice.

Two years later I published a book on the renewal of Cuba's revolutionary internationalism, which Fidel consistently championed in face of the trends and indifference of the times. In *La utopía rearmada: Historias de un viaje al Nuevo Mundo* (Utopia rearmed: Report on a trip to the New World, 2002), I told the story of the "fragile ones" and how Cuba launched the Comprehensive Health Program in Central America and the Caribbean, an initiative later carried out in many other countries.

A few years later, in 2005–2006, I crisscrossed Venezuela's cities, towns, shores, plains, mountains, and jungles, following the Cuban doctors and nurses who made—and make—possible Mission *Barrio Adentro* ("Into the neighborhood"). This experience led to the 2006 book *Venezuela rebelde: Solidaridad vs. dinero* (Rebel Venezuela: Solidarity vs. money).

During that trip I saw some of the best health-care professionals return to Havana to launch the Henry Reeve International Contingent of Medical Specialists in Disasters and Serious Epidemics. Starting in October 2014, members of that contingent confronted the Ebola epidemic in West Africa.

In March 2015, several months after the mission began, a small press team, which I headed, was commissioned to

go to Liberia, Sierra Leone, and Guinea. Hundreds of reporters had eagerly requested to cover the unfolding fight
against Ebola, and the wait was longer than we hoped for.
By the time we arrived, the Cuban mission had already
been completed in Liberia and Sierra Leone and would
soon end in Guinea. But the epidemic, while more under
control, remained active in all three countries—especially
in Sierra Leone and Guinea.

Until then, the only glimpses Cubans had into that mission came through Facebook pages kept by doctors and
nurses there. Ronald Hernández Torres in Liberia and
Enmanuel Vigil Fonseca and Luis Quiñones Aguilar in
Sierra Leone excelled in that voluntary and very personal
task. I was fortunate enough to be accompanied by two
Cuban television journalists of very different ages and personalities, both very professional. Tomasito "El Cangrejo"
(the Crab) Oliveros was an old-guard camera operator
and veteran of a thousand battles. Yordanis Rodríguez
Laurencio was a talented young man eager to grow. The
three of us, in fact, represented three different generations
of journalists.

I have tried to give this book the feel of a field report.
The reader will notice the author's personal perspective on the countries, participants, and events described.
But the backbone is the firsthand accounts by doctors,
nurses, scientists, officials, and government authorities
both from the countries visited and from Cuba, as well
as officials of the international organizations that were
involved.

The events and the accounts by participants are not presented in strictly chronological order but according to the
topics focused on in each chapter. Quotes not attributed
to publications have been transcribed from recorded con-
versations. Since it wasn't possible to give a biographical

sketch of each volunteer, I selected nine of them to give the reader an idea of the diversity of personalities the mission brought together for a common purpose.

The reader will also find references to articles of a more journalistic or scientific nature that appeared in Cuban and other publications, as well as to books and unpublished manuscripts. I quote from films I have seen, both fiction and documentary, that directly or indirectly address the issue of epidemics, particularly Ebola. And I add my own personal comments.

The book is not intended to be a scientific account, although it's based on the facts as seen by science today. It's a firsthand human and political account. I'm sure books of a scientific nature are being written by leading participants in this epic story and will appear along with other accounts by people who lived through every moment of the history recounted here.

I have included a good number of photos. I'm not and don't claim to be a professional photographer, although through chance and the good will of the Central Medical Cooperation Unit I was able to exhibit these photographs at the prestigious José Martí Memorial in Havana. I had a good camera with me and was in the right place at the right time.

The photos don't illustrate the disease itself. Above all, they depict the doctors and nurses of the Henry Reeve Contingent. Without their special protective suits, they are indistinguishable from other mortals. They touch death with their hands, but when they report for duty they make jokes that ease the tension and lift their own spirits as well as those of patients and colleagues from other countries. They are afraid, but they overcome that feeling to the point of forgetting it and becoming fearless.

Outside the "red zone," they record statistics, prepare

medications, and study. The red zone is the area with the highest level of contamination: patients presenting symptoms are isolated there until they recover or die. Doctors and nurses enter this area wearing hermetically sealed suits and must be carefully disinfected when they leave. The used suit is incinerated. Entering the red zone represents a moment of true dedication—a moment when brigade members perform their medical work and demonstrate their human virtues.

West Africa, specifically the three countries where the epidemic spread, became an immense red zone for customs agencies around the world. But the Cuban internationalists entered, exited, and cured patients, throwing themselves into this work. The color red was thus transformed into the symbol of a revolutionary tradition.

Cuban doctors and nurses flew in to Monrovia, Liberia; Freetown, Sierra Leone; and Conakry, Guinea, to fight Ebola. That's why we also took photos of residents of those cities. Not to depict their poverty or pain, like the stereotypical images in the unengaged and sensationalist press. The Cuban doctors went to give life, to restore hope, to affirm the human dignity of the peoples of Africa. Our reporting team went to bear witness to this.

When we arrived in Monrovia and Freetown, the Cuban doctors and nurses there had already concluded their work. We gathered their accounts and those of the authorities and health-care specialists, both local and foreign, with whom they collaborated. But we hadn't seen them at work in their medical centers.

It was only in Conakry that we found the Cuban brigade still immersed in daily work. There we were able to accompany its members as far as allowed by the perimeter established by strict norms of safety. We observed and photographed their work and shared their humor and fraternal atmosphere, their positive response to danger and tension. For this reason, most of the photos are of the Ebola Treatment Unit in Coyah, Guinea. Through those images we honor them all.

~

The list of people and institutions to whom I owe thanks is long. First to Rolando Alfonso Borges, who once again placed his trust in me, and to Roberto Montesino, who immediately gave his support to the mission. To the Ideological and the International Relations departments of the Communist Party of Cuba, which jointly supported this project. To the Ministry of Public Health and the Central Medical Cooperation Unit (UCCM), as well as to Cuba's foreign ministry.

On a personal note, I must thank my friends and co-workers Alpidio Alonso Grau and Yuliat Danay Acosta, who took on my daily responsibilities besides their own while I was in Africa, and then when I was immersed in researching and writing this book; they helped in reviewing the manuscript and selecting photos, respectively. Rosa Elena Encinas, a young journalist who, having recently started at the online Cuban publication *La Calle del Medio*, embarked on her work with great dedication and sense of responsibility. Julio César Sánchez Martínez and Idalmis Brooks, experts in international affairs.

My thanks to Doctors Regla Angulo Pardo and Iván Mora, director and deputy director of the Central Medical Cooperation Unit. Dr. Lorenzo Somarriba and his team at the health ministry's Center for Epidemiological Surveillance. And to Doctors Jorge Pérez Ávila and Salomé Castillo García from the Pedro Kourí Institute of Tropical Medicine (IPK). The former, the institute's director, is a distinguished scientist specializing in AIDS and Ebola; the latter provided scientific reports and expertise on Ebola, and was my first contact person both before I left and afterward during the quarantine period in Havana.

To Víctor Dreke, a leading participant in Cuba's history, comrade-in-arms of Ernesto Che Guevara during the capture of Santa Clara in December 1958 and in the Congo in 1965, as well as head of the Cuban military instructors and doctors who joined the combatants of the African Party for the Independence of Guinea and Cape Verde (PAIGC) led by Amilcar Cabral in the late 1960s. Oscar Oramas, Cuban ambassador to Conakry during those glorious years. Clara Pulido Escandell, head of the team responsible for Africa in the Communist Party's Central Committee. Ambassadors Maité Rivero Torres, Jorge Lefebre, Pedro Luis Despaigne, and Antonio Pubillones—guides, advisers, translators, all of them experts and lovers of Africa; the latter two were at the time chargés d'affaires in Liberia and Sierra Leone. Daffne Ernesto Mirabal García, third secretary of the Cuban embassy in Guinea.

Thanks to the heads of the three medical brigades— Doctors Jorge Delgado Bustillo (Sierra Leone), Juan Carlos Dupuy Núñez (Liberia), and Carlos Manuel Castro Baras (Guinea)—as well as their deputies, Doctors Luis Escalona Gutiérrez, Pablo Raventós Vaquer, and Graciliano Díaz Bartolo.

And to all other participants in this effort. To the translators of some of the documents I used as part of a basic essential bibliography: Inalvys Campo Lazo and Melvis Rojas Soris, from the team that produces *Panorama Mundial*, bulletin of the Communist Party's Central Committee. Cristina Híjar of Mexico, who sent me a very useful book on Ebola that had recently been published in her country. Mónica Orges Robaina, an editor and friend.

Daynet Rodríguez Sotomayor, my wife, who suffered every minute of my journey through the epicenter of Ebola, and who encouraged and supported me as my first reader and consultant in the process of preparing and writing this book.

AFRICA

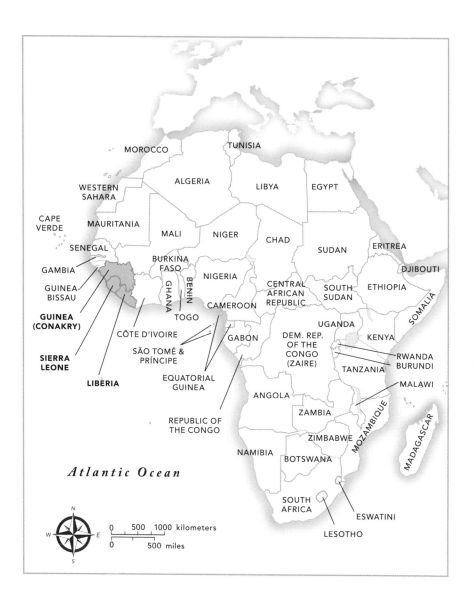

MOROCCO

TUNISIA

WESTERN
SAHARA

ALGERIA

LIBYA

EGYPT

CAPE
VERDE

MAURITANIA

MALI

NIGER

CHAD

SUDAN

ERITREA

SENEGAL

BURKINA
FASO

NIGERIA

DJIBOUTI

GAMBIA

GUINEA-
BISSAU

GHANA

BENIN

CENTRAL
AFRICAN
REPUBLIC

SOUTH
SUDAN

ETHIOPIA

GUINEA
(CONAKRY)

TOGO

CAMEROON

SOMALIA

CÔTE D'IVOIRE

UGANDA

SIERRA
LEONE

SÃO TOMÉ &
PRÍNCIPE

GABON

DEM. REP.
OF THE
CONGO
(ZAIRE)

KENYA

RWANDA
BURUNDI

LIBERIA

EQUATORIAL
GUINEA

TANZANIA

MALAWI

ANGOLA

REPUBLIC OF
THE CONGO

ZAMBIA

MOZAMBIQUE

MADAGASCAR

ZIMBABWE

NAMIBIA

BOTSWANA

Atlantic Ocean

N

W   E

S

0   500   1000 kilometers

0   500 miles

SOUTH
AFRICA

ESWATINI

LESOTHO

WEST AFRICA

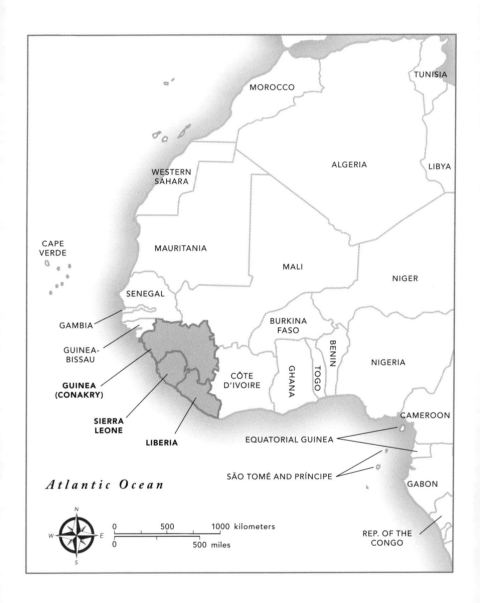

MOROCCO

TUNISIA

ALGERIA

LIBYA

WESTERN
SAHARA

CAPE
VERDE

MAURITANIA

MALI

NIGER

SENEGAL

GAMBIA

BURKINA
FASO

GUINEA-
BISSAU

**GUINEA
(CONAKRY)**

CÔTE
D'IVOIRE

GHANA

TOGO

BENIN

NIGERIA

**SIERRA
LEONE**

LIBERIA

CAMEROON

EQUATORIAL GUINEA

SÃO TOMÉ AND PRÍNCIPE

GABON

Atlantic Ocean

REP. OF THE
CONGO

N

W   E

S

0   500   1000 kilometers

0   500 miles

GUINEA, SIERRA LEONE, LIBERIA

SENEGAL

MALI

GUINEA-BISSAU

●Labé

●Boké

GUINEA

●Mamou

●Kankan

Coyah
Conakry⊕ ●Kindia
Wonkifong

●Faranah

Forécariah ⊕
Lungi

SIERRA LEONE

●Kérouané
⦿ Meliandou

Freetown ⊕
Waterloo⊕ ⊕

⊕ Maforki
●Port Loko

Kailahun

Guékédou

Kerry Town

Kenema

●Gbarnga

CÔTE D'IVOIRE

Monrovia ⊕

LIBERIA

Capital cities in bold
● City
⊕ City with Ebola Treatment
  Unit that Cuban doctors staffed
⦿ Suspected first case

Atlantic Ocean

N
W — E
S

0   100   250   400 kilometers
0   100   200 miles

The little killer returns

The epidemic threatened to spread.

United Nations secretary-general Ban Ki-moon understood that issuing a general appeal for help, without directing it to specific member states, wouldn't be enough. On September 9, 2014, he personally called the leaders of the three wealthy nations that had been colonial or neocolonial powers in the African countries now affected by the epidemic—the United States, the United Kingdom, and France. He also called the president of a small country that had fought alongside Africans for their independence in the second half of the twentieth century—Cuba.

EFE news agency reported from UN headquarters:

> The UN secretary-general telephoned several world leaders over the last few hours to request help for African countries affected by the Ebola outbreak, his spokesperson reported on Tuesday. The UN head spoke with, among others, Cuban president Raúl Castro, US president Barack

Obama, and French president François Hollande, as well as with British prime minister David Cameron and the president of the European Council, Herman Van Rompuy. The Korean diplomat thanked the leaders for their support in the fight against Ebola and "underscored the urgent need to increase it, including more medical teams, transportation, and funding to help communities affected by the epidemic," said his spokesperson, Stéphane Dujarric, in a press conference, according to EFE.

Ban also spoke with the president of Doctors Without Borders, Joanne Liu, whom he thanked for the organization's work and with whom he discussed how the international community can further support its efforts in West Africa.

Months later, professor Alpha Condé, president of the Republic of Guinea, who had taught at several French universities during the many years he lived in exile in France, commented to our small press team: "It was said that France would aid Guinea, Britain would aid Sierra Leone, and the United States would aid Liberia. But we have always asked for a worldwide response." That kind of distribution of aid would simply reproduce the historical colonial connections.

And why Cuba? The reason Ban Ki-moon—along with Margaret Chan, director-general of the World Health Organization (WHO), and the presidents of the three affected countries—asked for Cuba's help was evident: since 1963 Cuba's medical solidarity had reached almost every country on the African continent. At the time the Ebola epidemic broke out, a total of 4,048 Cuban medical volunteers, including 2,269 doctors, were working in 32 African countries, providing services in community health programs and hospitals. There were already 23 medical volunteers in Sierra Leone and 15 in Guinea. Worldwide, the small Caribbean island had a force of 50,000 health workers deployed across 66 countries.[1]

A decade earlier, Cuba had created the Henry Reeve International Contingent of Medical Specialists in Disasters and Serious Epidemics, which had worked effectively in countries as disparate and distant as Guatemala and Pakistan. Cuba was one of the few nations in the world that could mobilize large numbers of highly qualified healthcare workers.

"If we had the necessary sophisticated laboratories for the detection of Ebola in our country, the disease would not have spread," Alpha Condé noted during our interview, conducted in the presidential palace in Conakry. But in the beginning, he said, nobody knew for sure what we were dealing with. That came three months later, when the Pasteur Institute's laboratory in Dakar, Senegal, confirmed a patient's diagnosis. The exact origin of the first recorded case is unknown. Mexican anthropologist Miguel Ángel Adame Cerón gave the most widely accepted account:

> According to some sources, the current outbreak began in December 2013 in the village of Meliandou in Guéckédou, Guinea (ground zero), with the first infected members of a family (a two-year-old boy, three-year-old girl, their mother, and grandmother), who rapidly succumbed in December 2013 and January 2014.
>
> According to Fabian Leendertz, who led a November 2014 investigation by the Robert Koch Institute of Germany, there is a hypothesis that the child, Emile Ouamouno, was infected by bats of the *Mops condylurus* species, which are thought to have been natural hosts for the

---

1. Data provided by Cuba's health ministry.

hemorrhagic fever in previous epidemics and are able to survive infection with the virus. The report states that "children from the village played in a hollow tree trunk where bats from this species lived." The boy, whose symptoms were fever, black stools, and vomiting, died two days after being infected. The next death was that of his three-year-old sister Philomène.[2]

Emile had been unknown to the rest of the world. Could it be that a two-year-old boy in a Guinean village was the first rolling stone, one that snowballed worldwide? Could it be that the village of Meliandou, in the Guinean forest, with no banks or stock exchanges, with no internet, would alter the history of the planet? If the imprudent nurse who is said to have attended to Emile and Philomène had not gone in January 2014 to this village in Guéckédou district, near the Sierra Leone and Liberian borders, and started the chain of infections, perhaps these events would not have happened and this book would not have been written. These individuals simply didn't count—they didn't exist. The investigation into their final days was carried out almost a year after their deaths. "Civilized" people needed a name, a dark-skinned victim, a culprit.

On March 23, 2014, the World Health Organization made the Ebola outbreak in Guinea official, and a week later it confirmed a case in Liberia. A long time had passed since Emile and Philomène fell ill and died. But the official route did not include Sierra Leone, which announced its "first case" May 25. By then, the Cuban doctors in that country knew that the actual number of illnesses and

2. Miguel Ángel Adame Cerón, *Ébola y la mundialización epidémica* (Ebola and epidemic globalization; Mexico City: Ediciones Navarra, 2014), pp. 168–69.

deaths in that country was much higher. They had been working as part of the Comprehensive Health Program in remote communities of Sierra Leone, some in Kenema, a border district hit hard by the epidemic.

Cultural factors may have influenced the prevalence of the disease and how it became an epidemic. This was explained to me by Saran Daraba Kaba, a Guinean pharmacologist and anthropologist who was general secretary of the Mano River Union, a regional organization made up of four West African countries—the three affected by the epidemic plus Côte d'Ivoire. Leadership of the organization was then held by the Guinean government.

Kaba told me the border area where Guinea, Liberia, and Sierra Leone meet is inhabited by the Kissi ethnic group, which has its own customs and language, even though the official language of each country is either English or French. Moreover, the chiefs and their wives in these neighboring districts are related, constituting a clan. They are related in two ways: by tribe and by blood. This is the starting point for an ethnic group: common blood ties and belief in shared origins.

So the hypothesis mentioned earlier was plausible. Once a person became infected in Guinea, the virus could easily appear in Sierra Leone or Liberia within days. A sick person who didn't yet have symptoms would move around. From an ethnic point of view, they weren't leaving their nation or even family environment. "The epidemic must be confronted as a common problem of the three countries," Kaba insisted.

Liberia and Sierra Leone, however, were not prepared for this viral invasion. After more than ten years of civil war in both countries, their health-care systems, already precarious, were devastated. While it appears the first cases occurred in Guinea, over the following months the epidemic spread to the neighboring countries, causing more deaths.

Initially, opposition leaders were among those who died— they were from local parties that are ethnically based, as is common in Africa. Some said the government was hiding behind a nonexistent disease to selectively assassinate its opponents. But the facts demolished that claim—the virus was not at all selective.

Until then, the deadliest outbreaks had been the initial ones in 1976, which also occurred in countries sharing borders. The outbreaks were based on strains named after the affected countries—"Zaire," in what today is the Democratic Republic of the Congo, and "Sudan." The virus itself was named Ebola, however, after the Ebola river, which is close to where it was detected. It was the first time science had recorded the presence of this virus in human beings. Many doctors and nurses died because they were unaware of its deadly nature; they had simply followed their instincts in treating patients.

According to Dr. Jorge Pérez Ávila, director of the Pedro Kourí Institute of Tropical Medicine in Havana, in the initial cases the virus appeared as

> a jungle disease located in very small communities. Means of communication at that time were not what they are today, so these populations were often wiped out. Communities of 100 or 200 people would all die. There is a US film that tells the story: others arrive and find everyone there has already died.

That film is *Outbreak*, which we will refer to later (released in 1995, it was directed by Wolfgang Petersen and featured a host of stars: Dustin Hoffman, Rene Russo, Morgan Freeman, Kevin Spacey, Cuba Gooding Jr., and

Donald Sutherland). In it, the "bad" character is confident the virus will never reach citizens of the First World, noting: "It is the very lethality of this virus which works for us here. They don't live long enough to spread the thing around."

On that occasion, a total of 602 cases and 431 deaths were recorded from the different strains in Sudan and the Congo (Zaire). Subsequently the virus appeared in neighboring countries almost every year, but on a small scale. Five strains have been identified, with greater or lesser virulence. By 2014, close to 30 outbreaks had occurred in Sudan, the Congo, Gabon, and Uganda. The little killer, as many call it, lived entrenched in that area of Central Africa. (Adame Cerón, pp. 67–70)

In 1979 there was an outbreak among monkeys brought into the United States from the Philippines. The "new" strain, fatal to animals but harmless to humans, was named Reston, after the town near Washington, D.C., where it was first detected.

In 2013, however, the virus broke out unexpectedly in West Africa. It affected not only the three countries already mentioned—Guinea, Sierra Leone, and Liberia—but also initially Mali (eight cases, seven confirmed, and six deaths), Senegal (twenty cases, nineteen confirmed, and eight deaths) and Nigeria (a single case confirmed, where the patient recovered). Though it didn't spread in those countries, its presence was noted.

Jorge Lefebre, Cuba's ambassador to both Liberia and Sierra Leone, told me:

> In June 2014 I was in both Liberia and Sierra Leone as part of my usual schedule of visits. We were already concerned at that time. An epidemic was causing a rising number of deaths, although at that time it was a few dozen. But from

our knowledge of the previous Ebola experience in the Congo, it seemed to us that it had the potential to develop into what it eventually became.

At the time, the authorities had underestimated the scope of the epidemic. They were receiving no help. Africans were dying in remote regions. The disease wasn't reaching the cities, and they thought they could control it. That was in June. But in July, while I was in Cuba on vacation, the epidemic erupted, with those horrific numbers of deaths. The international press, too, contributed to creating a state of panic about a humanitarian catastrophe.

The ferocity of this new outbreak of the Zaire strain, the deadliest one for humans, can be seen in the triangle formed by these small coastal countries. The Centers for Disease Control and Prevention (CDC), based in Atlanta, posted on the internet a chronological map of the disease. In February 2015, a little more than a year after its detection in Guinea, there were already 13,855 confirmed cases and 9,004 deaths. Both figures would continue to rise, despite the significant reduction in the incidence rate.

By the end of August 2015, a total of 11,352 deaths had been reported, according to WHO. But this outbreak gave rise to a new development. The Zaire strain of the virus had now reached Europe—Spain, Italy, and the United Kingdom (one confirmed and treated case in each country)—as well as the United States (four confirmed cases and one death). Public health surveillance systems at these countries' borders were caught off guard.

This was something different, and panic ensued. Sensationalized press coverage blew the dangers out of proportion. But the fact remains that Ebola is a "hot" virus. It can destroy the body of any living thing within days and can be transmitted from one body to another through vital fluids. Some authors claim the damage AIDS causes in patients after a few years can be caused by Ebola in just a week.

Cuba responds

On August 8, 2014, eight months after the disease appeared in Guinea, the World Health Organization declared the Ebola epidemic in West Africa a "Public Health Emergency of International Concern." A few days earlier, WHO director-general Margaret Chan had contacted Cuban authorities through her representative in Havana. On August 13 the United Nations called for a global response to the crisis.

The Cuban government received an official request for help from the president of Sierra Leone, Dr. Ernest Bai Koroma, in an August 29 letter addressed to President Raúl Castro:

> It is with sadness, anxiety, and desperation that I write to you about the unprecedented outbreak of the dreadful Ebola virus that is ravaging our subregion and claiming the lives of many of our citizens including front-line health workers. This terrible scourge has created a health crisis of monstrous proportions that threatens peace, security and stability in Sierra Leone. . . .
>
> It is common knowledge that through your country's Cuban Medical Internationalism programme, medical personnel are sent overseas to assist with the delivery of health-care services. Indeed, Sierra Leone has benefitted from this type of collaboration to our satisfaction. I understand that it may be possible for Cuban specialists to come

to Sierra Leone to help with diagnostic tests and provision of clinical services geared towards fighting the disease.

As a true friend of Sierra Leone, I call upon you in this time of distress to use your good offices to assist us with the required specialists and technicians who will use their expertise to get us out of this serious health crisis. *[original English]*

Cuba immediately responded to the requests by the president of Sierra Leone and Dr. Margaret Chan. When the UN secretary-general made his phone call on September 9, three hundred doctors were already gathered in Havana and being trained at the Central Medical Cooperation Unit and the Pedro Kourí Institute of Tropical Medicine, where a complete model of an Ebola Treatment Unit had been built. The training was carried out by Cuban and WHO experts. It included a rotation through intensive-care wards in Cuban hospitals, a simulation of the conditions in field hospitals, and learning to use special protective suits.

The training was provided not only to those traveling to the affected region but to a group of medical personnel who, if necessary, would attend to cases that might develop in Cuba. Cuban volunteers who served in Sierra Leone said it was the Kourí Institute that gave them the basic training they would apply in their work; the instructors who were supposed to train them in Freetown didn't offer them much in addition. As one volunteer noted, using a sports analogy, "They were like fifth-degree black belts in karate who had never stepped onto a karate mat, or at most once or twice."

A delegation flew to Geneva September 10 to meet with Margaret Chan and her team. It was made up of Cuba's public health minister, Dr. Roberto Morales Ojeda;

Dr. Néstor Marimón Torres, the ministry's international relations director; Dr. Jorge Pérez Ávila, director of the Kourí Institute; and Dr. Jorge Delgado Bustillo, deputy director of Cuba's Central Medical Cooperation Unit, who had already been appointed head of the Sierra Leone brigade.

Cuba made its proposal before any other government, and it went well beyond what could be expected of a small, poor nation: 165 volunteers—62 doctors and 103 nurses. Included in this group were military doctors who wanted to join the effort. Out of the 256 health-care professionals who eventually went to the three countries, 23 were members of the Revolutionary Armed Forces. None of the military doctors went because they were given orders—they went as volunteers, and in a civilian capacity. Many of them had been part of the Henry Reeve Contingent since its establishment. Dr. Luis Escalona, a lieutenant colonel, confirmed this when he told me how he happened to be chosen:

> The hospital where I worked was offered two spots, and someone suggested my name. I was given a phone number to contact the head of the medical services department. When I called him he said, "We're looking for people willing to go to Africa and fight Ebola."
>
> I replied, "Sign me up."
>
> He said, "You could die in Africa."
>
> I repeated, "Sign me up."
>
> He added, "If you die, your remains will stay in Africa for five years and your family won't be able to see you."
>
> I told him, "Well, if I die, what will it matter where I am?"
>
> So he laughed and said, "I didn't expect anything less from you."

In addition, Cuba remained committed to maintaining the thirty-two brigades already working in African countries. The WHO director urged people to learn from the Cuban experience in treating emergency situations and thanked President Raúl Castro for Cuba's government being the first to respond to the international appeal for help. At a September 13 press conference held jointly with Dr. Morales and Dr. Chan, the Cuban health minister announced his country's decision.

After it was announced that Cuban volunteers were going to Sierra Leone, two more requests arrived. From Monrovia came a letter from Liberia's president addressed to the Cuban president. And in Conakry, the foreign minister, minister of international cooperation, and president of Guinea approached Cuban ambassador Maité Rivero Torres to request that a Cuban brigade come to Guinea.

The following are excerpts of the September 15 letter to Cuban president Raúl Castro from Liberian president Ellen Johnson Sirleaf:

> The virus is spreading at an exponential rate and we have a limited time window to arrest it. Well over 40 percent of total cases occurred in the last three weeks. . . . To break the chain of transmission, we need to isolate the sick from their families and communities, but this is impossible because there is nowhere to take them. We have been forced to turn back the sick. We are sending them home where they are a risk to their families and the communities. At this rate, Mr. President, we will never break the transmission chain and the virus will overwhelm us. . . .
>
> In a country that has barely emerged from a thirty-year period of civil and political unrest, with the presence of a large youthful (mainly unemployed) population, some of

whom were child-soldiers, this health emergency threatens civil order. What is even more heartbreaking is that we are unable to reopen our basic and secondary health facilities because terrified health workers, who have watched colleagues die, are afraid to return to work.

To date, about 153 health workers have become infected and 79 have died. There is now a recurrence of children dying of malaria because mothers could not find a health facility that would admit them. Diseases that were treated with relative ease pre-Ebola now take lives because of the pall that Ebola has cast over our health system. *[original English]*

The Liberian president asked that Cuba send disaster response medical teams to help direct the Ebola Treatment Units (ETUs) and medical personnel to restore basic and secondary health services in at least ten of the country's hospitals.

She concluded her letter with the following words: "Once again, dear brother, on behalf of the people of Liberia, I want to express our most sincere gratitude for the friendship and generosity of the Cuban people."

Ambassador Lefebre said he lived through some very intense moments as a diplomat:

While here, I simultaneously received official notes from the governments of Sierra Leone and Liberia asking that we please help them. They said we had well-trained medical assets and their citizens were dying.

That's when our president made a heroic decision—a decision that I imagine had to be evaluated down to the last detail of every aspect, because it involved many different things. This was a war. It meant sending doctors to fight not against bullets but against a lethal disease that was causing even more deaths than a low-intensity conflict.

Raúl, with courage and decisiveness that was true to our revolution's legacy of coming to the aid of the people of Africa, did not hesitate. He said: "Yes, we will help Africa."

For me, the night Raúl called was very emotional. He said, "We've weighed everything and we're going to help Africa. We need you to contact the presidents of those two countries, because tomorrow we'll make our decision public. We want you to inform the governments beforehand that we will respond to their appeal."

With the help of some friends I was able to speak with the two presidents. Their reaction, especially that of the president of Sierra Leone, was very moving. He told me, "I knew Cuba wouldn't abandon us. You are true to your heritage, to your African roots. That is what Fidel has taught you. I knew Cuba would continue to be a friend of Africa. Tell Raúl, tell the people of Cuba, that we will never forget that." Because at that time the situation was bleak. This was the second half of September. And on October 2 the first plane landed in Sierra Leone.

The Cuban government responded September 16 with the announcement that, in addition to the 165 volunteers to Sierra Leone, it would send 53 to Liberia and 38 to Guinea, the latter a country with which Cuba already had a long tradition of collaboration. Altogether, Cuba sent 256 health professionals to fight Ebola. Lefebre recalled:

At that point, no other government had yet decided to provide massive help against Ebola—everyone was afraid. Here there were medical teams of nongovernmental organizations, a few dozen doctors, some Chinese doctors who were already working in the hospital China had built in Sierra Leone. But no country responded as massively—or especially, as rapidly—as Cuba did.

In a phone conversation with the Cuban health minister, Margaret Chan thanked Cuba because the response had encouraged other countries. China expanded its medical team and donated another laboratory to Sierra Leone. European countries met to agree on an increase in economic aid (not on sending personnel). And President Barack Obama publicly announced that five hundred US soldiers would be dispatched to Liberia to build hospitals and other facilities.

Cuba was the only country that sent medical personnel. "The driving force for that international effort was Cuba," Lefebre told me. "The presence of Cuban doctors is what drew in the rest of the international effort."

The Cuban press published an extensive analysis by Fidel on October 2 entitled, "Heroes of our time," in which he noted:

Sending the initial medical brigade to Sierra Leone, one of the areas most affected by the cruel Ebola epidemic, is an example our country can be proud of. At this moment there can be no greater honor and glory. Just as no one has the slightest doubt that the hundreds of thousands of combatants who went to Angola and other African and Latin American countries gave humanity an example that can never be erased from human history, it cannot be denied that the heroic actions of the army of white coats will occupy one of the highest places of honor in that history.

It won't be the manufacturers of lethal weapons who attain such deserved honor. May the example of the Cubans marching off to Africa also take hold in the hearts and minds of other doctors around the world, especially those who have greater resources, practice one or another religion, or feel the deepest sense of duty about practicing human solidarity.

Those marching off to combat Ebola and for the survival of fellow human beings face a difficult job, putting their own lives at risk. We must continue to do everything in our power to ensure that those fulfilling such duties can count on maximum safety in their work and in the measures they must take to protect themselves and our own country from this and other illnesses and epidemics.

The personnel heading to Africa are also protecting those of us who remain here. The worst that could happen is for this epidemic, or more serious ones, to reach our continent—or the population of any country in the world where a child, mother, or any human being might die. There are enough doctors on the planet to ensure that no one has to die for lack of medical attention. That is what I wanted to say.

Honor and glory to our brave fighters for health and life!

The leaders of the Sierra Leone brigade left September 19 for Freetown. The heads of the Liberia and Guinea brigades left October 1 on the same flight taking the 165 volunteers to Sierra Leone. The remaining doctors and nurses destined for Liberia and Guinea left October 21.

A life-or-death gamble

The UN secretary-general's phone call to four world leaders, including the Cuban president, and Cuba's almost immediate response to the requests from the president of Sierra Leone and then the Liberian president and Guinean government, had a deep impact on Cubans, who understood the personal risks the volunteers would face. Hundreds of doctors and nurses spontaneously volunteered. The most competent were selected after the necessary medical checkups. The people of Cuba adopted those men as sons, brothers, and fathers.

I cannot say what a Cuban doctor—a critical-care physician with several missions under his belt—thinks or feels when someone shows up at his home, on his day off, and abruptly asks: "Are you willing to leave tomorrow for Liberia, Guinea, or Sierra Leone to fight Ebola, the most lethal epidemic humanity faces today? Will you risk your life for such a cause?"

But I can tell you what sometimes happens. The doctor accepts, and within three hours he packs and says goodbye to his parents, wife, and children. He joins others in Havana who have also accepted the mission.

One of these doctors remarked that some family members and neighbors called him a madman: "You're crazy! You could die!" But when he found out how many in his province had accepted the mission, he smiled—there were a lot of crazy people. And when he arrived in Havana, he told himself, "Well, Cuba is a country full of crazy people."

The counterrevolutionary press, which on a daily basis peddles values contrary to solidarity, tried to frighten members of the volunteers' families and Cubans in general. That second-rate press, whose raison d'être is above all to destroy Cuban solidarity at home and abroad, is capable of praising or understanding only the attitudes of those who think anything done for money is OK. They shamelessly insinuated that the internationalist doctors and nurses were forced to travel out of "material necessity." For cynics, this was reassuring, since such a heroic attitude and sense of history made their hair stand on end.

I can't say what a Cuban doctor thinks or feels when he decides to risk his life. But the following was the response of Dr. Iván Rodríguez Terrero, when he was interviewed by Yuliat D. Acosta for *La Calle del Medio* (issue 78, October 2014) during his training at the Pedro Kourí Institute before he went to Guinea:

> I'm aware we're going on a mission where there's no guarantee we'll return. That's hard on your children, but they feel proud. Your wife is sad because you're leaving, and sometimes a mission brings thousands of problems, but at the same time she feels proud. And when your children say, "My dad went on a dangerous mission, he had the courage to go!" it's an encouragement to your family.
>
> When they told us about Ebola, nobody asked, "Will they pay us?" That has never concerned me. Look, if I was interested in money, I would have said, "No, wait, I'm not going. I've already carried out some risky missions. I'm entitled to one that offers pay and better conditions." What's more, I was on sick leave. I have a fractured toe, which no one here knows about, but I said to myself, "I'm going!"

Then there's the response of nursing graduate Eduardo Almora Rodríguez, forty-two, whom I interviewed in Monrovia:

> Well, the mission was very risky. The media was reporting that. My family knew because there was a lot of news about it. My mom was in a terrible state when she heard me say I was going. She started to cry and kept saying, "Please be careful." But not once did she say, "No, don't go."

Unlike others who told me, "You're crazy, you guys are nuts, you're going to get yourself killed." Not my mom—she was always there, supporting me.

My kids, especially the eldest (twelve years old) told me, "Dad, take care of yourself, come back, you know you're heading toward death." He said it just like that—it gives me goose bumps! We were going and didn't know if we would return. Because it's not like they're shooting at you and you just hide. No, we didn't know where the bullet was! We knew the risks, and we needed that support.

The counterrevolutionary press continued to incite fear, expecting two major predictions to be fulfilled:
1. All foreign missions belonging to nongovernmental organizations—each consisting of one or two dozen health workers, never staying for more than six weeks—had suffered losses. So it was assumed that such a large group of Cuban volunteers, preparing to be in contact with patients for six months, would necessarily suffer the loss of many of its members. In the case of Doctors Without Borders, for example, nine out of sixteen health workers from that NGO had died from the virus as of October 14, 2014, as the Mexican anthropologist Adame Cerón reports in his book (p. 176).

The volunteers had accepted the medical guideline that if they fell sick they would be treated in the best centers available, and if they died their bodies would remain in Africa for five years before being repatriated. The media tried to use that to make families fear that the death of a loved one would be a double blow.

2. They assumed that the presence of so many Cubans in West Africa and the normal travel of passengers to Cuba, including university students from that region, would end up bringing the disease to the island.

Cuba counted on the opposite outcome, which to many must have seemed the least likely. We believed that both predictions would be proven false by our doctors' professionalism and discipline in adhering to the protocol in the red zone—and in the affected countries in general—together with Cuba's rigorous border screening. The volunteers themselves joked about the screening procedure, but the requirements were fulfilled without exception.

On October 18, 2014, the historic leader of the revolution offered a reflection that was published in the Cuban press under the title "Duty calls." Fidel wrote:

> Any thinking person knows that political decisions entailing risks for highly qualified personnel imply a high level of responsibility by those calling on them to carry out a dangerous assignment. It's an even harder decision than sending soldiers to fight and even die for a just political cause, something Cuban soldiers have always viewed as their duty.
>
> The medical personnel who are ready to go to any part of the world to save lives, even at the risk of losing their own, are the greatest example of solidarity that human beings can offer, above all when they are not motivated by any material interest. Their closest family members also contribute to such a mission by giving up a part of what they most love and admire. A country steeled by long years of heroic struggle can fully understand what I am saying.

A Central Group was created in Cuba's public health ministry, headed by the minister, Dr. Roberto Morales, to prevent the virus from entering the island, ensure the training of the Cuban doctors and nurses who would fight Ebola in West Africa, and analyze the available information on the epidemic. The group established a temporary public health surveillance unit of a more technical nature, with three teams of five. Each team had an epidemiologist, a biostatistician, a geographer, a computer scientist, and a representative of the Central Medical Cooperation Unit. The latter was included because volunteers from the Comprehensive Health Program were serving in two of the affected countries and Cuba had declared it would not withdraw medical personnel from any African country. A work schedule was established, with twenty-four-hour shifts followed by forty-eight hours of rest. Appointed to head the effort was Dr. Lorenzo Somarriba, an experienced epidemiologist who had coordinated the Cuban brigade from the Henry Reeve Contingent that fought the cholera outbreak in Haiti in 2010. Dr. Héctor Corratjé was his young deputy. The heads of the three brigades traveling to the coastal West Africa countries exchanged figures, information, and guidelines. As Dr. Somarriba recalled:

> We had precious little time to rest, as there could be no gaps, no margin for error. It was a matter of national security.
>
> We identified the main sources of information: the WHO Ebola Response Roadmap, International SOS, the Atlanta-based Centers for Disease Control and Prevention, and the European CDC. We used the government websites of the three countries where the disease continued to spread, as well as the websites of their health ministries. We installed a TV system with the main channels: CNN in English, TVE (Spanish television), South Africa's Africa Channel, other African channels, Russia Today, and teleSUR. We monitored them twenty-four hours a day, while working with the main administrative bodies of the Cuban government in charge of border surveillance.

When passengers arrived in Cuba, their travel over the previous thirty days was reviewed to determine whether they had passed through any affected countries. "We were in permanent contact with the Pan American Health Organization–WHO collaboration center. They gave us information and vice versa," Dr. Somarriba told me.

The moments of stress were experienced simultaneously in Havana and each of the three African capitals affected by the epidemic. The heads of the brigades immediately reported each incident, regardless of what time it was in one or another geographical location. Dr. Somarriba recalls with anguish the telephone ringing in his room during the early hours of the morning:

> There were some very tense moments. The most stressful, usually at night and often in the early hours, was when they called to tell you that a colleague in Africa had come down with a fever. If he had a fever, he had to be tested for Ebola and put in isolation. Those who had had contact with him were likewise isolated under a separate surveillance system. The hours it took, from the moment the fever was detected to when the test was taken and the results arrived, were agonizing.
>
> In some cases we had to wait more than a day. A young man from Ciego de Ávila—who I knew—had been put in isolation with a fever. He phoned to ask me not to tell his family. If he tested positive, he would tell me what to do. His request was met.

At the other end, in Africa, the tension was even greater. Dr. Delgado Bustillo, head of the Sierra Leone brigade, told me just a few days before his return, "I can tell you that every time I received a phone call after 10:00 p.m.

I was afraid. So I changed the routine, and from ten to eleven, I was the one who called everyone. We had seven cases of malaria. Today it's been sixty-seven days without any Cuban here coming down with fever."

Liberia

The airport in Monrovia is small, and the baggage-claim area a throng of impatient passengers. Rolando Vergara, in charge of logistics, greeted us before we passed through immigration and helped us identify our luggage. Waiting outside was Pedro Luis Despaigne, acting chargé d'affaires, who had arrived with our doctors and nurses to open a diplomatic office in Monrovia. He would be the person responsible for putting us in contact with the political world of the Liberian capital, and would serve as our translator. Cuba and Liberia already had diplomatic relations, but since the 1990s Cuba's ambassador had been resident in Accra, Ghana, and was accredited to both countries.

Earlier, we had passed through Charles de Gaulle Airport in Paris—all lit up, filled with moving walkways, rail shuttles, restaurants, and stores that opened up like carnivorous plants. Then we made a stop at the airport in Casablanca, Morocco, a human kaleidoscope: nowhere else in the world are passengers' dress and destinations so diverse and varied. At least three worlds intersect here—travelers from Europe, Arab countries, and sub-Saharan Africa. And in this case, three from the Caribbean and Latin America, who impatiently paced the large waiting room. Some of the airport walls displayed scenes of the city we would not be visiting, which were more beautiful and complex than the Hollywood studio image that fueled the romantic dreams of our grandparents.

But Monrovia is the capital of a small country. Its name honors US president James Monroe, the one associated with the Monroe Doctrine, which declared that all the Americas were for the (North) Americans. Liberia is a territory that—partly purchased, partly usurped by force—was colonized in order to "repatriate" freed slaves, as a compromise solution to the increasing number of free blacks in the racist US society of the early 19th century.

It should be kept in mind that, while an independent state was formally established in 1847, most of the Africans or descendants of Africans who arrived in Liberia from the United States were not originally from that region, and their presence too was imposed on the ethnic groups in that territory. In this sense, the United States imitated the British, whose ships had rescued Africans at sea from Portuguese and Spanish slave ships and brought them to Sierra Leone. That's why the capital of Sierra Leone is called Freetown.

The so-called Americo-Liberians are a powerful minority in that country. Coming from various African ethnic origins, in the 19th century they arrived in Liberia as English-speakers and with a culture influenced by aspirations and customs acquired in the New World. During their first decades in the newly established African country, they reproduced the manorial customs of the US South, now as the lords of Liberia. Even today, the children of the wealthiest Liberians usually attend universities in the United States. Representing about 5 percent of the population, they have higher levels of schooling and control the profits generated by the country's resources.

The Americo-Liberians exercised economic and political control for decades, after the agents of the American Colonization Society withdrew. The indigenous ethnic groups rebelled many times, but it wasn't until 1980, through a coup, that a representative of a local ethnic group became president. Of course, that doesn't mean the government was any better.

"It soon became evident," Cuban diplomat and scholar Clara Pulido Escandell wrote, "that the coup was a power grab. In the widespread chaos that ensued, conditions flourished for abusing power and looting the national treasury, which soon became rampant."* In 1989 a bloody civil war broke out. It ravaged Liberia for more than a decade, in two waves of conflict that lasted into the early twenty-first century.

Shortly after the war began, the neighboring government of Sierra Leone offered facilities to the joint military forces of the Economic Community of West African States Monitoring Group (ECOMOG), which were fighting Americo-Liberian warlord Charles Taylor in Liberia. Taylor responded by ordering his soldiers across the border to "neutralize Sierra Leone as a logistical base for the regional troops and to finance his own troops through the sale of diamonds from that neighboring country," as Cuban scholar Julio César Sánchez Martínez notes. As soon

---

* *Revista de África y Medio Oriente*, no. 1, 1996. See list of references at the end of this book.

as the flames reached Sierra Leonean territory, a huge fire was unleashed. Sánchez Martínez writes:

> The entry into Sierra Leone of an armed group from Liberia in late March 1991 was followed by a civil war that ended in 2002. While the troops' entry into Sierra Leone's southeast was a catalyst for the conflict, we cannot consider their presence the main cause of the war.

Following the approach of a Sierra Leonean historian, Sánchez Martínez lists the deeper roots of the war: political and social injustice, mismanagement, overcentralization of power and resources, poverty, illiteracy. In both countries, most youth were deprived of education or jobs. The lack of opportunities fueled a conflict with no political basis— one that soon left behind initial motivations or pretexts, imposed violence as a way of life, and used ethnic issues as a smokescreen. A ruthless struggle developed between its leaders for control of the illegal trade in diamonds. The warring groups became full-fledged criminal gangs that plundered and killed the peaceful residents of the villages they seized. When Ebola arrived, bringing its toll of death, the war was already over. But the health-care systems in both countries had been destroyed.

A long street runs through downtown Monrovia, from which the city spreads out. Burnt-out or half-collapsed government buildings and unfinished construction projects attest to the years of war. But people feared the epidemic more than the war. When the Cuban volunteers arrived, they found a ghost town. As Dr. Juan Carlos Dupuy Núñez, head of the brigade in Liberia, described it:

> We arrived October 4 and encountered a city that was virtually paralyzed. There was little movement apart from

the constant sirens of ambulances taking patients to hospital units or to the few existing Ebola Treatment Units, crammed with patients, that were run by Doctors Without Borders. It was a peculiar and dire situation in Monrovia.

Dr. Leonardo Fernández contrasted the early days to those we later witnessed:

> We found a deserted city. The streets were virtually empty of cars and people—there was no one in sight. Even in the hotel where we'd go for lunch and dinner, we saw only Cubans and three UN officials. And today, as we were just commenting, gentlemen, what a difference! So now we leave with a bit of pride, thinking: I did my part so this city would again be full of people.

Augustine Kpehe Ngafuan, Liberia's foreign minister, also referred to that early period in the discussion he had with our press team:

> In September and October, Liberia seemed like hell. It was as if the sky had fallen on our heads. Our people were dying on a massive scale. None of us knew what to do to survive. Cuba couldn't send money, as others did, but they sent their medical personnel and shared the risks with us. Their lives were in danger, but they didn't care. They said they were brothers who came across the ocean to help us.
>
> Now they're returning to Cuba, at a time when we haven't had any new cases for more than twenty-two days. If we continue like this, Liberia will be the first of the three most affected countries to be declared free of Ebola.
>
> But when the story is told of how we managed to overcome this disease, a major chapter will be devoted to Cuba and the role of the Cuban doctors. This is what will

remain in history. Cuba's actions are what makes our two countries feel closer, and what makes us feel love for that island.

The government anxiously waited the required number of days without new cases, as established by WHO, before declaring the territory free of the virus. The hotels filled up again, the streets were buzzing with pedestrians, and classes returned to normal.

Why was Liberia able to recover faster than its neighbors Sierra Leone and Guinea? Some argued that in Liberia religious institutions are not as influential as in other countries, so the state regulates questions such as funeral practices. The government organized safe burial procedures that had the support of the population.

In fact, whether or not a burial was carried out safely depended largely on a family's economic means, Dr. Pablo Raventós Vaquer, deputy head of the Cuban brigade in Liberia, explained. Digging a grave two to four meters deep requires adequate tools. As a result, many bodies were buried close to the surface, which meant rain could unearth them and animals, domestic or wild, could feed on them. If it was an Ebola death, the animal became a moving biological missile.

A system for the cremation of infected corpses was established. A December 9, 2015, *New York Times* article, however, captures the distress of the young people who worked in these crematories, which were hated and despised by the community:

> To understand how cremation is viewed by Liberians, one must first consider that this is a country with a national holiday—Decoration Day—meant solely for people to go and clean the graves of their loved ones. Every

year on Decoration Day, Liberians troop to cemeteries
and burial plots across the country with brooms, bleach,
soap, and water. . . . Many Liberians believe that if the
dead are not properly buried, they will come back to
haunt the living.

It was also reported that in the beginning, the national
army, supported by US troops, forcibly isolated infected
communities. This policy was later eliminated.

Leaning over the balcony in the back of the apartment
where Cuban doctors and nurses have graciously hosted
me, I can see the ocean. There's a beach, but the sand is
dense and the ocean swirls furiously a few meters away.
My hosts say that from this balcony they've seen whales
playing, and I lean forward waiting for a miracle that never
happens. The apartment complex has three buildings surrounded by high walls with barbed wire at the top—as
do almost all the affluent homes and buildings across the
city. These are luxury apartments designed for temporary
guests, mostly Americans, hosted by well-financed NGOs
or international organizations.

In contrast, between the ocean and the apartment
complex there are two or three blocks of moldy tin roofs,
under which another kind of life is throbbing, barely
visible from the outside. When night falls, the shacks
merge into an undifferentiated blur, separated by distant
street lamps. On one side, however, the John F. Kennedy
Hospital, a private facility, can be seen. It's only partially
functioning because it's short of staff, and construction
of one of the wings was never completed because of the
civil war.

When the Ebola epidemic broke out and gravely ill people began to arrive, the hospital collapsed. Many doctors
and nurses died from the disease and others left. The epi-

demic struck terror in the medical staff, who were caught off guard and unprepared. Dr. Pablo Raventós recalls:

> A man had driven up to the entrance to Kennedy Hospital and died inside the car. He was left there for three days. People looked at him but didn't dare touch him. His head lay on the steering wheel. We saw it from a distance. When we arrived, dead bodies were in the street. They were fumigated, but we were told, "Don't touch. Don't help anyone. We know how you Cubans are. Don't come to anyone's aid. And on the slightest contact, use the 'weapon'—the sanitizer. Don't hesitate to pour it on you." When we went out we would ask each other, "Did you bring the weapon?" And if we had left it behind, we'd go back for it.

The US weekly *New Yorker* reported in its August 11, 2014, issue, "The hospitals of Monrovia, the capital of Liberia, are full of Ebola patients and are turning away new patients. . . . Infected bodies are being left in the streets: the outbreak is beginning to assume a medieval character." But Adame Cerón corrected the latter assertion: the epidemic, he said, had assumed a neoliberal character.

When I look out from the balcony on the other side, the landscape is different: comfortable houses and apartment buildings similar to the one we're staying in, all surrounded by walls and barbed wire. The owners are Lebanese. As Dr. Pablo explains:

> The accommodations were negotiated directly with the Lebanese, with lawyers involved, and we're not used to that. We thought we were going to arrive at a facility and they would tell us, "You're going to sleep and eat here." But instead we had to negotiate, accompanied by lawyers and

a WHO representative. We visited many housing facilities until we finally found the three we needed.

Twice a day, however, the inevitable blackout happens—in these homes it's very brief because the generator immediately kicks in. Then there's another problem: the city's water supply. Most residents get up early every morning to fetch it from nearby wells.

We wander through the streets looking for the building that had housed the Cuban embassy before the armed conflict began. It seems to have been a two-story mansion with spacious gardens. We picture it as it might have been, but what we find is a burnt-out, half-collapsed house—who knows whether due to a stray mortar shell or looters?

I walk through the door of an outer wall that was no longer standing and discover people inside. Some men shout angrily at us from the opposite sidewalk. My companions approach them and explain. The ruins of the house evidently provide shelter for families that have made it their own. An occupant hastily explains that the house used to be another country's embassy. Several blocks further down we find another house that appears to be what we were looking for. This one seems to have had fared better, although the walls block our view of the inside. It now houses a US NGO. The guards don't allow us to look inside.

I am careful not to judge. We're overloaded with false images that television, movies, and more recently the internet surreptitiously project on our retinas and shape what we see. It's not that these images are entirely false, but they create lasting stereotypes. When we look for a preconceived image, camera in hand, we're looking without seeing. I want to find the human beings who inhabit the city. To understand the doctor, you have to understand the patient. On the streets, many people protest angrily when we take out our cameras. Africans are fed up with arrogant photographers, foreigners who come to snap pictures of poverty and turn the human beings who inhabit this continually plundered and humiliated continent into a mere part of the landscape. They're tired of being exotic objects for foreign visitors who couldn't care less.

Ebola Treatment Unit/ Defense Ministry

The Ebola Treatment Unit where Cubans had worked was no longer operating when we arrived in Monrovia. It was located in front of a half-built, burnt-out building originally designed for the defense ministry, an uncompleted donation from the Gadhafi government in Libya. We visited the ETU, where a group of Liberians was practicing the process of putting on and taking off the special suit, a vital safety procedure required to enter the red zone. Today, unfortunately, a new confirmed case of Ebola was announced in Monrovia. The borders with the countries affected by the epidemic are porous.

The unit is a field hospital, similar to others in basic design but with some unique features. Field-hospital wards are usually made of canvas, but this one, built by the Chinese, is a small hospital with the latest technology, including a TV system for monitoring patients. Cuban volunteers in Liberia helped build the center where they worked, making adjustments to the original project. Dr. Pablo Miguel Raventós Vaquer explained:

> We visited several treatment units, and no two were alike. Nobody knew how the ideal Ebola Treatment Unit should

be set up, so everyone had their own conception. The Doctors Without Borders group had built one, the Americans another, and the Chinese another.

Back in Havana several months later, I studied a plan of the Liberian center and compared it with the one in Coyah, Guinea, to which we did have access. In the Monrovia unit, which was still fully operational, we wouldn't have been able to photograph or film from the green zone the work being done within the red zone. A central hallway in the forbidden-access zone separated two wings with patient wards that were mirror images of each other, although only one wing became operational. The doors to the red zone led to the inner hallway, not to the green zone. The wards were divided into small cubicles.

The advance team—Doctors Dupuy and Raventós; Andrés Marrero, responsible for finances; and Rolando Vergara, in charge of logistics—arrived October 4 in Monrovia. Two days later they visited the center for the first time, with construction in full swing. Dr. Raventós, and then the epidemiologists, made suggestions on the structure and the flow of patients and doctors, which were accepted.

"Working with the Liberians and the doctors from the African Union was a very positive experience," Dupuy told me. "We worked in a treatment unit where the collaboration and solidarity were exemplary." The preliminary training, carried out in Cuba at the Pedro Kourí Institute, had been meticulous at every stage. "The teachers there trained us very well," Eduardo Almora Rodríguez told me. But in Monrovia, he noted, the training with patients took place at the center itself:

Phase three was very important, because we completed it here in the ETU with patients. I had the honor of being

the mentor for the Cuban nurses, together with Dr. Os-
many, who was the mentor for the doctors, and we had
to train the whole group. It was a beautiful experience
because it involved working directly with Ebola patients.
The first day we went easy, but as typical Cubans, by the
second day we already wanted to start an IV. I would tell
them, "Easy does it, we'll do that later." We went step by
step. We trained well.

The nurses' accounts are eloquent. Reinaldo Hernández
Fuentes, 41, from Santiago de Cuba, recalled:

The first few days there were forty-two or forty-three patients. Walking into the treatment unit, we saw the room
was full. It was tough. We knew that patients were going
to die at some point, that they couldn't be saved. We saw
them pleading for their lives, but we couldn't do more
than what we were doing. Every day when I arrived, I
wanted to run to the ward for confirmed cases, to see how
the boy or girl I had cared for on the previous shift was
doing. When you managed to get the patient through the
fifth or sixth day, the chances of survival were 70 to 80
percent. And to see a seven-year-old boy, a twelve-year
old girl, a young woman of eighteen who we've saved—it
gives you immense joy.
   I've kept some photos. There was a child who lost his
mother, father, and brother—he was alone. We also saved
the eighteen-year-old who looked after him in the room,
and she adopted him.

It was a disheartening, unequal struggle. The nurses and
doctors were prepared for intense days, and they worked
hard. The reward of a life saved, however, did not always
come. It was the worst thing that could happen to these

men who were so willing to give all—the feeling they were working in vain. The first memories of Ricardo Zamora Álvarez de la Campa, a nurse from Pinar del Río, were sad:

A child arrived in an advanced stage of the disease, and there was practically nothing you could do. You went into the treatment unit, and he was already dead. These were hard blows, and what always came to mind were our own kids, who were nearly the same ages: four, five years old. We were able to save many, but many also died. It's a very difficult experience. It will always remain etched in my mind, in my memories of this mission.

The nurses were the heroes of this story. Leonardo Fernández talks about their role:

Those I really admired for their courage were the nurses. There was a series of rules—taboos—in the books on what you couldn't do, on what you couldn't touch. You couldn't insert a Levin tube [catheter]. You couldn't approach a patient who was bleeding. The first to break through those barriers were the Cuban nurses.

Dr. Somarriba, who was in charge of the health ministry's Provisional Working Group for monitoring Ebola in Havana, told me a wonderful story about the kind of medical care needed for hemorrhagic fever:

Ebola is a hemorrhagic fever, and we Cubans have experience in treating this kind of fever. Not Ebola, but dengue fever, and the mortality rate for dengue in Cuba is very low. We know how to treat it. There's no specific treatment for these diseases—it's supportive care. You have to touch the patient. Professor Armando Caballero, one of our best intensive care specialists, once told me, "Treatment of dengue is *encimático.*"

I asked, "*Enzimático* [enzymatic]? Please explain, I don't know anything about that."

He replied, "*Encimático* with a 'c.' You have to be *encima*—on top of the patient."

In the treatment center they had put up a tree of life. It was a tree where black ribbons were hung every time someone died and colored ribbons for each person saved. The same was done in the Maforki–Port Loko Center in Sierra Leone. Dr. Fernández recalls, "It was very comforting to see that as the days passed, the tree of life was covered more and more with red, blue, white ribbons, the colors of life." When the Cubans arrived, the fatality rate was 90 percent. When the final assessment was done, before their departure, the fatality rate—deaths from confirmed Ebola cases—had fallen to 45 percent. Ebola had almost disappeared from the country.

It was difficult to assert that "it was gone," however. The disease would reappear July 1, 2015. By August of that year, six more confirmed cases and two deaths had been reported. On September 3, 2015, WHO again declared Liberia "free of Ebola." But the killer was still at large, lying in wait, and it soon showed up again. On November 20, 2015, three new cases were reported.

The men I

Tracing the footsteps of the Henry Reeve Contingent

DR. JUAN CARLOS DUPUY NÚÑEZ

Dr. Dupuy has a distinguishing trait: everyone says he speaks "British" English. A clinical lab and health-care management specialist, he taught himself English because he likes the language and loves the music of the English-speaking world. This and his organizational abilities led him to become the founding coordinator of the Henry Reeve International Contingent of Medical Specialists in Disasters and Serious Epidemics.

The contingent was created by Fidel in September 2005 to aid residents of the US city of New Orleans after it was ravaged by Hurricane Katrina. The contingent's name expressed the goal of building bridges of solidarity. Henry Reeve was a courageous New Yorker who enlisted in Cuba's nineteenth century independence war against Spanish colonialism and gained the rank of general. He died in combat at the age of twenty-six.

Dr. Dupuy had previously served in Eritrea, in northeastern Africa, from 2001 to 2004, as head of a medical brigade of forty-six volunteers. There he organized the Comprehensive Health Program and opened the first medical school, where Cuban instructors taught the courses in English. Called to Havana in 2005 when the contingent of 1,500 doctors and nurses was organized, he was asked to coordinate an intensive program to train them in epidemiology and working in disaster situations. It was a wonderful period, marked by extensive meetings with Fidel.

The Henry Reeve Contingent was officially constituted September 19, 2005. But US authorities rejected Cuba's offer of assistance. "Fidel told us not to become discouraged. He said we should return to our jobs and be ready, because the contingent could go into action at any moment," Dr. Dupuy said. The following month Hurricane Stan hit Guatemala, devastating twelve of its twenty-two states. That was the inaugural mission:

> I remember that I left on the second flight. Six flights took a total of six hundred volunteers out of the original fifteen hundred members of the Henry Reeve Contingent. We aided the victims of the heavy rains and mudslides. A lot of people died or were left stranded. As you would expect with floods and heavy rains, there were outbreaks of epidemic diseases: acute respiratory illnesses, skin and diarrheal diseases, and so on. We had the opportunity of providing support with an array of medicine we carried in our backpacks to ensure essential primary care for storm victims. From the beginning, the contingent worked as a self-sufficient medical unit.

Three months later Dr. Dupuy was called back to Havana. An earthquake had mercilessly rocked Pakistan, a distant land with which Cuba had few ties. Because of his expertise and command of English, he was again chosen for that mission.

The experience in Pakistan was wonderful from a medical and professional standpoint. First we were in Islamabad, then we went to Abbottabad. Of the 44 units deployed, 32 were field hospitals, and it was decided to transfer the command post from the capital to Abbottabad, which was closer to the epicenter. We had a major field hospital in Muzaffarabad, another in Mansehra, and one in Abbottabad. They were three large flagship hospitals, with a total of 2,474 members of the contingent working in them. As the Henry Reeve Contingent grew in number, it also grew in experience.

I was the coordinator there for seven months, from start to finish. We were able to care for more than 1.8 million patients, and performed a good number of surgical procedures, deliveries, and pediatric consultations. A select number of amputees were sent to Cuba so they could receive prosthetic devices.

In 2006 Dr. Dupuy returned to Cuba. The following year an earthquake struck Pisco, Peru. Because of his experience, he was asked to go there to set up Cuba's field hospitals in the disaster zone and then return home. But he ended up staying another four months. From 2008 to 2011 he worked in Nigeria, leading a small group that designed and built an ophthalmology center.

He smiled when I asked how he was contacted about joining the brigade that would confront Ebola in Liberia. He was about to leave for Saudi Arabia, on what is known as a "compensated" mission, when he got a call from the Central Medical Cooperation Unit: "Are you willing to join the Ebola undertaking?"

I learned to value the revolution from outside Cuba

DR. LEONARDO FERNÁNDEZ

Fernández, at sixty-three, is one of the oldest doctors on the Ebola mission and the younger volunteers look to him. His discreet appearance offers no hint of his youthful days as a long-haired, rebellious rock fan. But something gives him away, perhaps his smile, or his mischievous eyes with faint lines that crinkle when he speaks.

It was in Nicaragua that I became a revolutionary. Earlier, when I was seventeen, you couldn't listen to Beatles songs or go to a bar or be out on the street late at night. And although my family had belonged to the July 26 Movement, and my father and sister had been in the Sierra Maestra mountains, I was a rebel. I didn't understand. I liked rock music and had long hair. But I had been educated in the principles of the revolution, and one day I was told: "There's this situation developing." I raised my hand and off I went. And I learned to appreciate Cuba. It was outside Cuba that I learned to value the revolution.

That was his first mission, in 1979. It was a month after the victory of the Sandinista revolution in Nicaragua. Sandinista leader Daniel Ortega assigned him to be the personal doctor for Steadman Fagoth Muller, who later became a leader of the *contras*, and he lived in Puerto Cabezas, eastern Nicaragua, until 1981.

When he told me this story I remembered that in 1999

I had interviewed Fagoth at his ranch by the Coco River. He had spoken about the Cuban doctors—about the one who in Nicaragua had provided him with good care, free of charge. And about the doctor in the United States who had charged $18,000 for an operation.* Later, back in Cuba, Dr. Fernández specialized in intensive care and internal medicine. He didn't travel again right away. "I never signed up for the placement lists for international volunteers. It seemed absurd to me. Until Fidel called for doctors to go to the United States after Hurricane Katrina. I was among the first hundred fifty selected. Then the brigade grew to fifteen hundred." He'll never forget the moment when Fidel spoke to them in the Ciudad Deportiva sports arena in September 2005.

The US government, however, didn't accept the offer. Then, with the subsequent earthquake in Pakistan and floods in Mexico and Guatemala, also in 2005, the contingent was divided into three groups:

> I was assigned to go to Pakistan with an initial group, mostly military doctors and some civilians with a certain degree of experience in such situations.
> While I was still in Pakistan, [Cuba's then-deputy foreign minister] Bruno Rodríguez asked if we were willing to continue directly on to East Timor [in the Pacific, east of Indonesia]. I was among those who said yes. I raised my hand thinking I probably wouldn't go because I was about to return to Cuba, but they chose me. I was in East Timor for two years.

---

* Enrique Ubieta Gómez, *La utopía rearmada: Historias de un viaje al Nuevo Mundo* (Utopia rearmed: Report on a trip to the New World; Havana, Casa Editora Abril, 2002), pp. 66–67.

Then the earthquake in Haiti struck [in 2010], and they called for volunteers. When it comes to volunteering, I raise my hand first, then I ask what for. In Haiti I organized the intensive-care field unit.

After that he still had time to carry out a "normal" mission in Mozambique, for two years. The most difficult test would come with the Ebola epidemic. Yet he plays down the importance of what he did:

Look, the widespread media coverage this mission received—the propaganda that spread through Facebook, across the internet—has made some of us think we've done something extraordinary and see ourselves as heroes. I believe we simply fulfilled our duty. We upheld ethical values as revolutionaries and doctors.

What's the difference between us and our compañeros working in the Brazilian jungle? Or those in the Venezuelan jungle, working for months in remote indigenous communities? What's the difference between us and those working in villages across Africa?

I'm lucky to have gotten to know parts of Africa. I lived, for example, in the capital of Mozambique, working in one of its intensive-care units. But there were compañeros who lived on the border, in the jungle, with temperatures of 48 degrees Celsius [118 degrees Fahrenheit]. . . .

What's the difference? The difference is that this was a well-known international mission. It received media attention. It was given the importance it deserves. Because it's undeniable—you really do have to have guts to say "I'm going," and to confront it. But it was just one more assignment.

I had heard about Ebola, I'm familiar with Africa. I had helped combat hemorrhagic fever in Mozambique. So I raised my hand and here I am. Nothing special. It's life.

As long as I have the strength and they accept me, I'll go wherever I have to go.

Life doesn't go around twice

DR. ÁNGEL ENRIQUE BETANCOURT CASANOVA

Dr. Betancourt was born in Central Havana, but his family moved to the San Isidro neighborhood of Old Havana, where the legendary pimp Alberto Yarini operated in the early twentieth century. Now Betancourt lives near Obispo Street. He has a certain way of talking, and I would say a certain way of life, because he's a man from the barrio, from his barrio. But I too lived in Central Havana, so I don't find his expressions and mannerisms odd.

Make no mistake—at thirty-seven he's a doctor and pediatric specialist. He has a six-year-old son. And a father who is no longer around but who is always with him. I ask about his father, and before answering Dr. Betancourt says: "How should I talk to you—in Spanish or Central Havana Spanish?" "However you want," I reply.

My dad was one of the people I most respect, even after his death. Why? His example. And because while in Liberia I found out that one of the members of the Medical Commission was a student of my dad's. My father was doctor to Samora Machel, the president of Mozambique. The plane in which Samora Machel was traveling was attacked, and my dad died [in October 1986]. Just like that. My dad was a good person. A good doctor. What more could you ask for? He was forty-two.

Enrique—some call him Kike for short—was in Angola from 2010 to 2012, working at the Luanda General Hospital as a pediatrician. "It was a little complicated," he tells me. "A lot of poor people needed us, a lot of rich people took advantage of us. Angola? It wasn't about money. What stays with you is how large people's needs were, and how much we were able to do for them."

I asked him how he came to enlist in the war against Ebola:

I got a call, and my wife told me not to say yes. Everyone knew—but I had a history, I am the way I am. If my dad died when and where he did, why wouldn't I go? I have to do my part. Maybe I'm crazy—I'm not like anyone else. My wife wasn't happy, my mom wasn't happy, they've been crying every single day.

This is a suicide mission. You guys [the press team] just arrived here and you don't feel worried. When you head for Sierra Leone, that's when you'll realize how worried and stressed you've been. The group we have is incredible—you feel safe knowing you have two or three brothers here. That's the most important thing. The rest is learning to live in this situation created by the disease.

The head of his unit, Dr. Pablo Raventós, a colonel and director of Havana's Naval Hospital, where Betancourt works, told the story from his vantage point:

Kike is a civilian worker in the Revolutionary Armed Forces. I sent for him. I told him, "Look, I called for you, not for you to go fight Ebola, but for both of us to go. I can assure you that if you accept, we'll go together." He

"We are certain that there will be no lack of volunteers for Algeria. That more will step forward, as an expression of solidarity with a fraternal people who are worse off than we are."

—Fidel Castro, 1962

CIENCIAS SOCIALES

"It's hard to find an African country that has not received assistance from our small island," says Enrique Ubieta.

Top: Ernesto Che Guevara (second from left) with Cuban volunteers in Algeria, 1964, Cuba's first internationalist medical mission. Today some 50,000 Cuban health-care volunteers are serving in more than 60 countries.

Bottom: Cuban doctor (left) trains students as he treats patients during liberation struggle in Guinea-Bissau, which won independence from Portuguese rule in 1974.

"The decisive victory of the Cuban people in 1959 became an example of what a small nation can do for others while fighting for itself."

— Fidel Castro, 2014

PASTOR BATISTA/GRANMA

Top: Conakry, Guinea, March 1976. Fidel Castro with African leaders as Angolan and Cuban forces routed first invasion of Angola by South African apartheid regime. From right, Agostinho Neto, president of Angola; Castro; Ahmed Sékou Touré, president of Guinea-Conakry; and Luis Cabral, president of Guinea-Bissau.

Bottom: Luanda, Angola, January 1989. Crowds bid farewell to internationalist combatants returning to Cuba. From 1975 to 1991, 425,000 Cuban volunteers answered request by Angolan government to help defend country from repeated South African invasions.

Top: Southern Bolivia, December 1966. Ernesto Che Guevara, third from left, with part of guerrilla unit that sought to forge a fighting movement of workers and peasants that could open the socialist revolution in South America.

Bottom: Havana, March 1990. Cuban president Fidel Castro welcomes children who were victims of 1986 nuclear disaster in Chernobyl, Ukraine, as they arrive in Cuba. Over the course of twenty years, Cuba's medical personnel cared for 25,000 children and others affected by the radioactive blast.

"Because we have revolutionary power, everyone in Cuba receives medical care."—Enrique Ubieta

GRANMA

BOHEMIA

In Cuba working people made a socialist revolution. They took state power, overturned capitalist rule and property, and built new social relations. Millions transformed themselves in the process.

Top: Peasant receives title to land he works following Cuba's May 1959 agrarian reform law.

Bottom: Telephone worker chisels name off formerly US-owned Cuban Telephone Company, August 1960, part of nationalization of imperialist-owned enterprises by Cuba's working people and their government.

Left: Cuban literacy volunteers on way to teach in rural areas, early 1961. Hundreds of thousands learned to read and write. Within a year, illiteracy had been effectively wiped out in Cuba.

GRANMA

Right: Field hospital in territory held by revolutionary forces led by Fidel Castro, eastern Cuba, late 1958. During struggle against Batista dictatorship, Rebel Army clinics gave free treatment to peasants and combatants alike, including wounded government soldiers.

YALE UNIVERSITY

Left: Birán, eastern Cuba, 2016. Resident gets checkup as family doctor visits rural households. Quality health care at no cost to patients is available to all, made possible by Cuba's socialist revolution.

In the US, dog-eat-dog capitalist relations force individual families to shoulder responsibility for social needs such as medical care, which tens of millions can't afford.

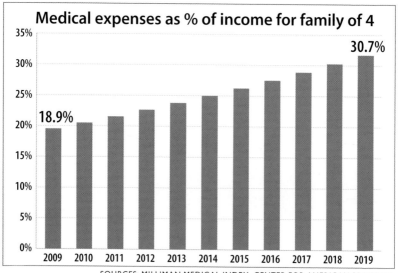

Medical expenses as % of income for family of 4

35%

30.7%

30%

25%

18.9%

20%

15%

10%

5%

0%

2009 2010 2011 2012 2013 2014 2015 2016 2017 2018 2019

SOURCES: MILLIMAN MEDICAL INDEX, CENTER FOR AMERICAN PROGRESS

Top: Hundreds line up before dawn for free dental care at a two-day clinic in Salisbury, Maryland, 2017. Many, like Dee Matello (foreground), had not been able to afford dental care in years.

Bottom: Rising medical costs are eating up more and more of working people's income.

Top: New York, March 2019. Hundreds of nurses rally outside Mount Sinai Hospital during contract fight. They demanded more nurses be hired. Understaffing, they said, means higher profits for hospital owners but worse care for patients.

Bottom: Brookwood, Alabama, October 2015. Members and supporters of United Mine Workers union protest gutting of pensions and medical benefits for retirees and widows.

"Just as Cuban combatants in Angola gave an example that can never be erased from history, the heroic actions of Cuba's army of white coats will occupy a place of honor." — Fidel Castro, 2014

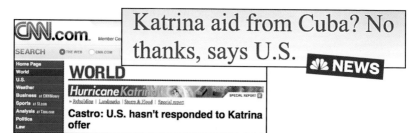

Katrina aid from Cuba? No thanks, says U.S.

NBC NEWS

CNN.com

SEARCH ○ THE WEB ○ CNN.COM

Home Page
World
U.S.
Weather
Business at CNNMoney
Sports at SI.com
Analysis at Time.com
Politics
Law

WORLD

Hurricane Katrina

» Rebuilding | Landmarks | Storm & Flood | Special report   SPECIAL REPORT

Castro: U.S. hasn't responded to Katrina offer

Top: Havana, September 2005. Some 1,500 members of Cuba's Henry Reeve medical contingent, their backpacks filled with supplies and equipment, ready to fly to Louisiana to aid those needing care after Hurricane Katrina. Washington flatly refused.

Bottom: After US officials rejected Cuban help, Henry Reeve Contingent flew to Pakistan to aid earthquake victims. It has since provided emergency medical care in dozens of countries.

JUVENAL BALÁN/GRANMA

answered, "Let me go get my bags ready." I said, "No, wait, wait. Not so fast, there's a checkup." And he reiterated, "I'm going to get my bags to go with you." It was as quick as that.

So he signed up. We were lucky that life threw us together in Liberia. He was the only pediatrician in the brigade, and there were many children with Ebola. He even established guidelines for the treatment of children with Ebola, which we wrote up, printed, and made available to all units. That was Kike. With his Central Havana ways, you wouldn't imagine what kind of person he is.

When Kike paused for a moment in telling his story, I needled him. I said there were people asserting that the Cuban doctors were here for the money. He looked at me for a few seconds without saying anything.

When they called me—I was called by my director, who is also my compañero, and I hope Pablo will now become my friend—I was on duty that day. I don't know why people say those things, why they get into those arguments. I was on duty that day, and he told me, "Hey, Liberia, Ebola, what are you going to do?" And I said, "I have no problem with that, I'm off to fight Ebola." And that was without knowing how much I was going to earn. We spent almost two months in the Central Medical Cooperation Unit.

Anyone who wants to listen, let them listen. Do you know when I found out how much I was going to earn? Here in Liberia, when they paid me my stipend, twenty-one days later. So, who is it that's trying to discredit us? Who's saying that?

"In a few years you'll be the age your father was when he died," I told him.

"Yes, pretty soon. And so what?" he replied. "Life doesn't go around twice. You only live once."

Sierra Leone

The international airport serving Sierra Leone's capital is located in the Port Loko district, on the north side of a wide bay. On the opposite shore, not visible across the water, the city of Freetown awaits. To get there you have to drive around the bay on roads, often unpaved, that are permanently jammed with vehicles. Depending on the traffic, the trip can take three to four hours. The other option is to cross by water.

The ferry wasn't running when we arrived; the Ebola epidemic had put a halt to the service. It's probably not the same ferry Fidel took on May 7, 1972, with then-president Siaka Stevens, during a brief visit just after diplomatic relations were established. But there was a relatively comfortable though expensive boat ($40 per passenger for a one-way ticket) that got us to Freetown in twenty-five minutes.

We were welcomed at the dock by Antonio Pubillones Izaguirre, Cuba's interim chargé d'affaires. As in Monrovia, he had opened a diplomatic office here after the arrival of the Cuban doctors; the ambassador was based in Accra. Pubillones would serve as our liaison and guide to Sierra Leone's political scene, as well as our translator.

In the city, affluent homes are interspersed with houses made of mud or tin; paved streets with roads of dirt or mud, depending on the season. The streets are filled with cars and even more street vendors, carrying baskets, crates, buckets, or trays on their heads with the most varied wares. The public minivans pass by, jam-packed with passengers indifferent to the danger of direct contact with a carrier of the virus. Everything is smaller, more concentrated, perhaps, and some downtown buildings have a definite air of the "British tropics."

We stayed at the Leisure Lodge Hotel, which faces the sea. To get there from the main road, we took a narrow dirt path that curved like a hook. Lined with shacks that seem less than promising, it takes you to the gate of the small two-story hotel, inexplicably preceded by almost luxurious private homes.

Inside the second-floor hotel room, a huge mosquito net hung over the bed, and the old air conditioning unit was working. There was a small balcony overlooking the sea and a vacant lot, but I didn't dare open it—the mosquitoes, dangerous enemies, lay in wait. Some of the Cuban doctors and nurses had stayed at this hotel when they first arrived.

The city, undeterred, had not retreated from its daily bustle, though the epidemic was still claiming an average of seven people a day. Other diseases, with a longer history, were taking a higher death toll. People didn't seem to fear this game of dice. The epidemic had subsided, and people were resuming their lives. Dr. Jorge Delgado Bustillo, however, recalls the impact of the early days:

> When we arrived, the figures ranged between a hundred and two hundred cases a day. On September 26 I entered

one of the first hospitals that had been set up here, at the police academy, for treating Ebola. It had a hundred beds, all of them occupied, and not enough staff to care for all the patients. I found patients dead in their beds. Some patients had fallen off the bed and were on the floor; others were crying out for something.

I entered the hospital, wearing full protection, to see the environment where my people would be working. All the Cubans walked through this treatment center, suited up and hands clasped, as part of their psychological adjustment. There were three phases: theoretical, simulation, and practical. We carried out the simulation phase at that hospital, with fifteen trainees a day. They passed through but didn't touch anything—they observed, remained for an hour, and left. Then we checked the disinfectants, the chlorine solutions.

Dr. Rotceh Ríos Molina, a specialist in internal medicine, twenty-nine, was designated to guide his colleagues through the simulation visits. Together with Dr. Felipe Delgado, an epidemiologist and twin brother of Jorge, and Dr. Manuel Seijas Gutiérrez, subsequently appointed coordinator of the Maforki–Port Loko team, Dr. Rotceh had been part of the visits to two of the three Ebola Treatment Units in Freetown and was familiar with those facilities:

At that time there were only three functioning centers. One, with local staff, had been set up at the police academy as a site to care for Ebola patients; two doctors there had already fallen ill. Another was run by Doctors Without Borders and had the best hygienic conditions and medical care.

The third was a holding unit, to "hold" patients until they were confirmed as positive or negative. But many clinical and epidemiological errors were made—they put confirmed patients in with the unconfirmed, and when a negative result was reported, that person had already become infected there and released onto the street, widening the chain of transmission.

The holding unit was in a place called Newton, in the outlying metropolitan area, about forty-eight kilometers [thirty miles] from Freetown. It was a primary school where they had removed the desks and set up some beds. But the patients were all kept together—both positive and negative cases—and samples took a long time to come back from the lab, often up to seven days. It was a disaster.

We didn't visit the Doctors Without Borders center. They didn't establish relations with the Cubans, although later we took part in some meetings with them and exchanged experiences.

The government enforced sporadic curfews, and checked the temperature of drivers and passengers at key points in the city and surrounding areas. Every time you entered an establishment you had to wash your hands in a tank of chlorinated water. Sometimes measures were more drastic. According to Adame Cerón:

> On November 27 Sierra Leone ordered a three-day closure of all stores and markets (except pharmacies) in Freetown, the capital. Mayor Sam Franklyn Gibson asked people to wear long clothing and avoid personal contact with others as much as possible to reduce the chances of contracting the virus through sweat. (p. 179)

In Sierra Leone, as in Guinea, there weren't enough labs. The Ebola test results could take days, which didn't help in eradicating the epidemic.

Six months after the Cubans arrived, the situation was still unsatisfactory, as Dr. Delgado explained:

> Last week there was an average of four or five cases a day—some days eight, others zero. But it all depended on the diligence of the laboratory, which might have a backlog of twenty samples and give you results the next day. The positive samples might have been sent to the lab three or four days earlier. That was a serious problem, which was gradually lessened with the addition of twelve more labs. There was one in Kerry Town, established by the British health ministry. South Africa also had a very good one, and the Australians another one. The Centers for Disease Control and Prevention of Atlanta also had a lab in the Kenema area. Then GOAL, an NGO, established one near Port Loko.
>
> Prior to that, samples from Port Loko were sent to the capital for diagnosis. Some samples would break or results of tests would not be reported—there was a serious lack of controls. The country was simply not prepared for the epidemic.

Two of Freetown's most attractive features are the beachfront—unlike Monrovia, where the shore does not seem to be part of the life of the city—and the mountains, which are dotted with buildings. Both Freetown and Monrovia lack a basic water distribution system and sufficient electricity generation capacity. In years just prior to the epidemic, Sierra Leone's rate of economic growth had been relatively high, among the highest in Africa, especially given the low level from which it started—it was considered one of the poorest countries in the world. But Ebola halted and reversed this trend. Investors fled.

Dr. Samura Kamara, Sierra Leone's foreign minister, told us somberly:

Ebola is the second crisis to hit this country in recent years. An eleven-year war had ended in 2002. Just as we were moving forward, developing, like a normal country, Ebola hit us in May 2014 and did a lot of harm. We've fought from the start, and fortunately the international community came to our aid. We are very grateful to the government and the people of Cuba for sending a huge medical contingent, which was made available to us from the beginning. It has helped us contain Ebola in our country.

All economic projects were paralyzed because companies canceled their contracts. Sierra Leone's finance minister, Kaifala Marah, said in October 2014 that the Ebola crisis was producing the same effects as an "economic embargo." Adame Cerón wrote, "An October 13 report described the following situation: in the entire area affected by Ebola, stores remained closed, hotels empty, flights canceled, crops left untended, investments halted." (p. 191)

Near us was Hotel Mariam, where a large group of Cuban volunteers and their "general staff" were housed (it was already customary for Cubans occasionally coming here to stay in this hotel). It wasn't luxurious, but its employees went out of their way to provide attentive service. Dr. Jorge Delgado recalled:

> We started training in groups at the Hotel Mariam. We brought volunteers in from the Compañero, Barmoy, and Seaside hotels. But there were few instructors. Teresa, a professor from Barcelona, came to Hotel Mariam and taught groups of twenty at a time, and that dragged out the training period. While all this was happening, negotiations continued with WHO and the Sierra Leone

health ministry to determine where we would put people to work.

We didn't rest until our compañeros got used to wearing the PPE [Personal Protection Equipment] as their regular outfits. We requested a large supply of suits from WHO. We first did the training in each hotel, hidden inside the rooms so hotel guests wouldn't be frightened. But you had to wear the suit for two hours a day, every day, even on Saturdays and Sundays. I reported this to Cuba, and eventually I was told to let people rest on Sundays. Each volunteer underwent a rigorous process to be certified by WHO in the use of the protective gear. Sometimes they did something wrong, got nervous, so the exercise was repeated. Everyone was aware of the risks.

Ebola Treatment Units in Sierra Leone

In contrast with Guinea and Liberia, where the number of Cuban volunteers was only enough for a single unit, in Sierra Leone the 165 Cuban health workers were distributed in large groups across several facilities. They were stationed at the Kerry Town, Maforki–Port Loko, and Waterloo ADRA Ebola Treatment Units. They also worked at the Ebola observation center of the Ola During Children's Hospital, which sent confirmed patients to other centers.

It wasn't until a month later that the British Ebola Treatment Unit in Kerry Town opened, in a rural neighborhood near the Waterloo area. With eighty beds, it was run by an NGO called Save the Children, headed by a retired colonel. The facility included a hospital section with twenty beds run separately by the British navy for its own civilian and military personnel. Following the protocol, Cuban patients with fever were also treated in that section. Among them were Reinaldo Villafranca Lantigua and Félix Báez Sarría. "They went through a lot of stress until their Ebola results came back negative," Delgado told me.

Despite initial reservations, Save the Children expressly requested that Cuban medical personnel work with them. Dr. Delgado recalls:

> They knew—either from what they had heard from others or from their own experience, I don't know which—that the work done by the Cubans would be good. Maybe not in terms of ability to communicate in English, but certainly in medical expertise. We gave them the list of our people, they made their selection, and the Cubans trained right there. I should say the Save the Children personnel learned at the same time as we did, since they had a lot of pediatric experience but not in this kind of work.

Based on the number of patients treated and lives saved, the two units that did the best work were unquestionably Kerry Town and Port Loko. The former had perhaps better conditions, while the latter was right in the focal point of the epidemic. "Kerry Town was the flagship—they worked round-the-clock, in six-hour shifts," through March 9, 2015, Dr. Delgado told me. "At the other three sites, by decision of the authorities, we covered the 8:00 a.m. to 8:00 p.m. shift."

The Kerry Town unit officially opened November 4. Attending the ceremony were the nation's president, top WHO authorities in Sierra Leone, Save the Children, and the Cuban ambassador. From then on the Cuban flag was flown at the facility alongside those of Britain and Sierra

Leone. Dr. Ramiro Guedes Díaz coordinated the group working there. He went into the red zone of an Ebola hospital more than any other member of the Cuban brigade. We visited the Kerry Town unit and interviewed the British director, Andy Mason, who was very sad the Cubans were then about to leave:

> When you're working with Ebola everything is tough, especially if you haven't done it before. What we did was bring together different groups to work effectively: Save the Children, the Cuban brigade, the British department of health—all those working in the British government lab—and later, our brothers and sisters from Sierra Leone. But the key to our response capacity was the Cuban brigade. They were the heart of the response here.
>
> I don't think that citing figures—how many lives have been saved, how many survived, how many died—is the most appropriate way to talk about the fight against Ebola. But in my humble opinion, this is the best Ebola Treatment Center in the world. I'm confident—and I'm not a doctor or epidemiologist—that our figures will show how much the fatality rate has been reduced. That wouldn't have been possible without the diligent care for the patients. And our Cuban colleagues were vital in that patient care.

The last question we asked, intended for Cuban television viewers, was what message Mason wanted to send the Cuban people. His reply was emphatic: "The first thing I would say to the Cuban people is: Thank you for making available the excellent nurses and doctors we've had. The second is: If possible, in the future please make these doctors and nurses available again to work with Save the Children, anywhere in the world."

Forty-two Cuban volunteers—twenty-five nurses and

seventeen doctors—were stationed in Maforki–Port Loko. The Ebola Treatment Unit had 106 beds. During their stay the Cubans treated 499 patients (a high percentage of whom were confirmed cases) and saved 132 lives. "More than three lives saved per volunteer," Dr. Manuel Seijas González, the Cuban team coordinator in that unit, told me with evident pride.

The Port Loko district is a very poor rural area, with little infrastructure and few jobs. Electricity is a modern amenity available only to those who can afford to install generators, which provide power at least at night. Before Ebola appeared, a hydroelectric plant was being built on the river, but the project ground to a halt. Nearby the iron ore mines were abandoned. There are no water treatment facilities. The only water sources are the river running through the town and a few wells. Even having a well is a luxury. Most houses are made of adobe bricks. Dr. Seijas is pleased to have headed up the Cuban team in that district:

> Before we arrived in Port Loko, the fatality rate was 90 percent. Patients believed that going to a treatment center meant going to your death. This was turned around while we were there. Within a month or so we managed to reduce deaths by almost half. Patients began asking to be treated at the sites where the Cubans were.
>
> Our center became a reference point—the lowest fatality rate in the district. This was thanks to the efforts of each of our compañeros. The group came together quickly and worked with discipline and dedication.

To determine where Cuban brigade members would be placed, Seijas along with Doctors Felipe Delgado and Rotceh Ríos visited the centers that were functioning. "The first time you walked into a center, it was a tense moment," he said. "You were facing an unknown, a very lethal virus, an enemy you couldn't see. We'd look around and ask, 'Where is it?'" he said, smiling.

There was a tree of life at this center, too. Moments before his return home, Carlos Reyes, a nurse, recalled: "Our tree, a little mango plant, was in front of the center. Every time a patient was discharged, especially a child, a colored ribbon was tied to a branch. We ended up covering the tree almost completely with ribbons of life, even the topmost branches."

The Waterloo ADRA treatment center was located in a small rural community. The name has nothing to do with the history of Africa—it refers to a British military victory in 1815 best remembered for the stature of the defeated leader, Napoleon Bonaparte. Waterloo ADRA will not be remembered as the site of a defeat, however. There death was confronted, combated one on one, and statistics took on a human face. The fight began and ended with each patient. Nurse Juan Carlos Curbelo recalled something that also happened at other facilities:

> This was a government center with minimal resources, not at all comparable to Kerry Town. In the holding center intended for unconfirmed patients, there was a pregnant woman diagnosed with Ebola. She needed a transfusion, but the hospital didn't have the money to buy blood bags. Dr. Rotceh asked us to make a collection, with everyone putting in what they had at that moment—ten or twenty thousand leones. Each blood bag cost $40 to $45, at five thousand leones to a dollar.
>
> We collected the money, bought the two bags, and gave her the transfusion. The head nurse at the hospital told us it was useless, that the woman was going to die anyway. But we couldn't fail to do everything in our power to save

her. After a few days she did die, but we were at peace with our conscience.

Saving a life—even one—was important. This particular center was designated for the care of pregnant Ebola patients; seven of the beds were reserved for them. The facility was a Seventh-Day Adventist hospital—in Cuba it would have been called a clinic. It provided minor surgery, laboratory work, and imaging services. The government rented it when the epidemic began. It had sixty-six beds: ten divided equally between a tent for suspected cases and one for probable cases. The ward for confirmed patients had fifty-six beds. It was in turn divided into two areas, one for the most serious cases and one for those recovering.

The first institutional delivery of a child of an Ebola patient in Sierra Leone was conducted there, under the supervision of Dr. Elionis Escobar Rojas, a surgeon from Havana's Finlay Hospital, and Dr. Juan Andrés Morells, a gynecologist from Santiago de Cuba. Although the delivery was successful, the patient and baby later died from Ebola complications.

Dr. Rotceh Ríos Molina, head of the Cuban medical team at the center, recalled:

> When we arrived, the center had no supplies and was closed. There were thirty-seven compañeros and me, thirty-eight altogether (twelve doctors and twenty-six nurses). We found two local doctors, the director of the center, and twelve nurses. We agreed on schedules and work procedures. We made a few suggestions to modify the center's layout to improve health and hygiene. This included changing the entry and exit paths so that each was one-way.

On December 20 we began to work and saw the first five patients. We worked in six-hour shifts, 8:00 a.m. to 2:00 p.m. and 2:00 p.m. to 8:00 p.m. Each shift had a doctor in charge and a second doctor. Two Cuban doctors and three nurses. Six nurses each day. With this roster, people rested seventy-two hours between shifts. The Cubans took on the bulk of the work. The Sierra Leonean nurses followed the instructions of the Cuban doctors.

The Cubans taught the Sierra Leoneans many procedures. We inserted Levin tubes and IV catheters. When patients were very dehydrated we put in a double IV. We administered enemas. We did digital rectal exams on patients with bowel obstructions. . . . And we established a norm that was followed everywhere in Sierra Leone: There were no differences between doctors and nurses. Everyone had to perform IV insertions, wipe bottoms, and mop up vomit. In fact, this norm was carried out to the letter.

The Ola During Children's Hospital in Freetown, the only such hospital in the country, received suspected cases and maintained a holding center. Patients waited there for lab results, so their degree of illness could be classified and they could be relocated to other centers. The Cubans worked every other day in teams of four—two doctors and two nurses. The shifts were twelve hours at first, later reduced to eight. The coordinator of the Cuban team in the hospital was Dr. Luis Darío Castro Basulto.

Víctor Lázaro Guerra Viera was one of the nurses assigned to the Ola During Hospital. The youngest Cuban brigade member in all three countries, he was twenty-five when he arrived and turned twenty-six while in Sierra Leone. *El Niño* (the Kid), as his co-workers called him, worked as a pediatric nurse in Cuba. "My team was special," he said. "There were two of us from Pinar del Río, one from Matanzas, and one from Havana, and we kidded each other a lot about baseball. The four of us are baseball fans," he said.

In a more serious tone, he told me:

> Closing a child's eyes is very hard, especially when you have children of your own. But the important thing was, even at that critical moment in their illness, to make sure they felt they had someone at their side giving them support, and that's what we did. We gave them stuffed animals and other little toys so they wouldn't feel alone. I'm grateful for this mission because it was very important.
>
> One day I was called to see a child who needed an emergency IV in order to receive a blood transfusion. None of his family members wanted to donate blood, and the family didn't have money to pay for the transfusion. So we pooled some of our own money, paid for it in the hospital, and got the blood bag. We were able to help that patient. We didn't know yet whether he had Ebola. He was fitted with an IV drip.
>
> When I arrived at the hotel where we were staying, I was told the boy had tested positive for Ebola, but his life was saved thanks to what we had done at that moment. When I went back to work two days later, he was already laughing, and he recognized me. It was a beautiful experience. When he left the hospital we hugged, and I even have a picture with him. That was a very special case.
>
> Another experience was very hard for me. There was a seven-day-old baby who was dehydrated, and his mother had been transferred because she had Ebola. Can you imagine—just seven days old! In Cuba, neonatal pediatricians are the only personnel authorized to give an IV to such a young baby. For me it was a unique experience. I asked God to help me find that child's vein, and I only had

to give him one prick. Thanks to God and to the IV I gave him, we saved his life.

Unfortunately his mother died, and so did his father. The boy had no relatives so he was sent to an orphanage. Such a small child. He was like so many other kids—like a seven-year-old whose life I saved who had no family.

We sometimes had entire families admitted. We might save two or three, but the others would die. Or the whole family died—mother, father, children. It was very hard, much more so for me because I work with children.

A few hours in Lungi

Last night we said good-bye to our hosts in Freetown. In the early afternoon we took the boat back across what is one of the largest natural bays in West Africa. Before leaving, on the small pier Dr. Delgado bought me a book in English about the history of Sierra Leone.

There was still a long wait in the town of Lungi, Port Loko district, where the international airport is located. Dr. Amaury Domínguez, from Santiago de Cuba, and Luis E. González Arias, a nurse from Las Tunas, who had been told in advance that we'd be there, took us to their home, far from the pier, town, and highway. They were serving in Lungi as part of Cuba's volunteer Comprehensive Health Program brigade.

The house, surrounded by the usual protective wall, was spacious, though it lacked some amenities. Electricity was a luxury that the Cubans saved as if it were water, which was also scarce. They had a generator but used it only during the hours when it was most needed. They generously shared with us their only two fans.

Luis, in charge of the kitchen that day, went out of his way to make us a farewell dinner. We talked; there wasn't much else to do. Only one TV channel was available, and they had already watched all their videotaped films five times. When they get home from work, they have routines they follow: exercise, water the garden, do the laundry, cook, think up other chores.

These were two men living in an isolated, rural part of Africa, in the midst of a serious public health situation. It wasn't safe to go out. The house had a custodian, or rather two, who rotated day and night shifts. There was also a driver, who lived in town and came when called. Of course, they missed the women members of the Comprehensive Health Program brigade, who had returned to Cuba when the Henry Reeve Contingent arrived.

Like the women who had been there as medical volunteers, these men had not come to Sierra Leone to fight Ebola, but were now confronting it. Each of them, however, had been hit twice with malaria. Dr. Amaury told me the second time it dragged him down and he lost a lot of weight, but he recovered. I lent him my cell phone so he could call his wife in Santiago de Cuba. The phone had been given to me by Dr. Dupuy, head of the Liberia mission, at the request of the health ministry when we said goodbye in Monrovia.

We didn't sleep that night. At 3:00 a.m. their driver showed up, and we tried to leave for the airport in the car they normally used. But this time it wouldn't start. In the darkness of the African night, three journalists and two health workers pushed the car, but it refused to take us. The driver, from Lungi, who had given me two CDs of music he said young people in his country listen to, called a friend who drives a taxi. The taxi got us to the airport.

The men II

'The Prof'

DR. JORGE DELGADO BUSTILLO

Some called him *El Profe* (the Prof). Between internationalist missions, some lasting a few months and others, years, Dr. Jorge Delgado Bustillo, an epidemiologist, justly prided himself on having built up a number of risky missions in his cache of memories: Angola, Nicaragua under the first Sandinista government, Zimbabwe, South Africa, Guatemala, Honduras, Paraguay, Sierra Leone. He had been part of efforts to combat or prevent epidemics in countries hit by hurricanes, earthquakes, and civil wars.

But now he was confronting Ebola, a raging virus. The disease didn't require a natural or social disaster of the kind described by the news media in order to spread. Rather, it relied on an "invisible," permanent catastrophe: poverty.

Dr. Delgado was a deputy director of Cuba's Central Medical Cooperation Unit. He had been assigned to attend an important meeting of the working group created by the health ministry to prevent the epidemic from entering Cuba. His experience and his command of English— or rather, lack of inhibition in speaking it—made him an ideal candidate to lead one of the brigades preparing to leave for Africa.

The leadership of the health ministry supported the proposal that I head the upcoming brigade, and I immediately accepted. I accompanied the minister of health to the first meeting in Geneva. Néstor Marimón, the ministry's international relations director, and Jorge Pérez Ávila, director of the Pedro Kourí Institute, also attended. We met with Margaret Chan, and the minister introduced me as the person selected to go to Sierra Leone.

If I remember correctly, we arrived back in Cuba on Sunday, September 14. On Monday we were already meeting with the brigades that were being organized. I took part in the physical exams and dental checkups at the Hermanos Ameijeiras Hospital, the Guanabacoa dental clinic, and the school of dentistry. On Thursday, September 18—I remember well—I traveled to Sierra Leone along with Dr. Rafael Corona and Francisco Benítez, who was responsible for the brigade's finances.

Dr. Delgado was the oldest among the heads of the Cuban brigades in the Ebola triangle. His outgoing, hyperkinetic personality makes him seem to be in perpetual motion. He speaks loudly and emphatically, so it's hard not to notice his presence. He acts boldly and confidently in the most complex situations. He has a twin brother, Felipe, also an epidemiologist, who like him has joined hazardous international missions, and who lives and works in Cienfuegos. Both went to Sierra Leone.

The two brothers enjoy taking advantage of their physical resemblance. Felipe replaced Jorge as head of the Cuban medical mission in Zimbabwe when Jorge was appointed head of the group working in South Africa. Like two kids, they spent the first days of the transition period in Zimbabwe surprising the authorities. First Felipe would walk in and everyone greeted him as Jorge. Right after that Jorge would show up, just to confuse them. But the brothers' experiences in Sierra Leone cannot be compared to their earlier ones. Never has Jorge so feared—and perhaps never will again—for Felipe's life. His brother was one of the two men who had unprotected physical contact with the only Cuban who fell ill with Ebola. Jorge prefers, however, to talk about the early days:

We arrived September 21. It was Sunday and the city was under curfew. We settled in at the medical volunteers' residence and talked with Dr. Eneida Álvarez. She had until then been head of the Comprehensive Health Program brigade and she gave us a lot of information. I had instructions from the health minister to take charge of all the work of the medical volunteers, which she understood perfectly.

The next day I went to the public health ministry and to WHO. They already knew I was coming, and I began arranging to find housing for the large group of 162 volunteers who would be arriving, plus the three of us.

We had to move fast. The country was depressed and the hotels were empty. Not every place had the basic safety and comfort we were looking for, but we succeeded. When our colleagues arrived October 2 at 10:20 a.m., we had a place for them to stay.

Orula's blessing

ORLANDO O'FARRILL MARTÍNEZ, NURSE

Orlando lives in the Cerro neighborhood of Havana, three blocks from the Esquina de Tejas intersection. His house is spacious but in need of repairs. The paint is peeling. When you enter the living room, you immediately notice that this is the home of a practitioner of one of the Afro-Cuban religions. Orlando has a nursing degree and is an intensive-care specialist with twenty-five years' experience. He is also *Ni Orunmila*, a *babalawo* (which means "father of the secrets") registered with the Cuban Yoruba Association.

He had passed the English exams required in certain countries that have cooperation agreements with Cuba and that, having greater material resources than other countries, offer doctors more favorable living and working conditions. He was going to join a Cuban medical mission in an oil-producing country, possibly Qatar or Trinidad and Tobago. But Ebola intervened. He remembers clearly the day and time: "They phoned me September 2 at 11:00 p.m. to ask if I would accept the change of destination." He said yes.

It was a mission for our homeland, but I had to consult with my *orishas* [deities]. They gave me permission and told me everything was going to turn out fine. I'll be honest with you. I live with my grandmother, who is 102, and with my mother, who is 75. I didn't tell them I was going to fight Ebola. They knew about my decision to go on a mission to Qatar or Trinidad and Tobago, but they knew nothing about the Ebola mission. I left in secret. They're learning now of the scope of the decision I made.

Exactly a month after that phone conversation, O'Farrill left for Sierra Leone. Because of his experience, his command of English, and his specialty in intensive care, he was selected to join sixty doctors and nurses making up the Cuban team in Kerry Town—the first ones to become part of the effort.

But he wasn't just an outstanding nurse—he was also a babalawo. "I was always praying for the health of our co-workers, so we'd all come back alive," he said. "Unfortunately that didn't happen—two compañeros died [of malaria].* But the orishas didn't forsake me, nor did I forsake them." Before long, other Cubans started seeking him out. He inadvertently became the babalawo of the brigade, just as the British had their chaplain. He left Cuba prepared for this, as the orisha Orula had told him to be. Among the Cuban health workers, as among the Europeans, there were both believers and nonbelievers.

On their first day in Kerry Town, as the bus took them downtown, they were astonished when they looked out the window and saw Cubans in their special suits helping sick people who were lying in the gutter. There they saw Dr. Félix Báez. Earlier they had watched in horror as a sick person crawled along the road in the direction of the field hospital. Difficult days were in store for the brigade.

Orlando did his work, his *ebbó*, so that Doctors Luis Escalona and Felipe Delgado, who had been with Félix when he first contracted the illness, would not be infected. "Remember, we're Cubans, it's in our blood," he told me, smiling. "And I wanted to help with the religious part. I

---

* See chapter "Those who fell."

consulted, and Orula gave me the answer about what had to be done—we call it ebbó—to clean him, to clarify things, so everything would turn out well." Apparently it worked.

Orlando was called to the bedside of our co-worker Reinaldo Villafranca Lantigua, "Coqui," who came down with cerebral malaria. But his condition worsened very quickly. The British navy chaplain, too, prayed for his soul during the funeral. I remember that Víctor Lázaro Viera, a nurse, had told us:

> We pray when we go in, in order to feel a little more protected if they're watching us from up there, to give us the strength to carry on and contain the disease. We help and always watch out for each other. We pray for those who enter the red zone and are tending to patients, risking their lives. We pray for everything to turn out well.

Orlando told me about the children he could and couldn't save. About the indifference or paralyzing fear in the beginning that dehumanized the treatment of patients. About how the Sierra Leonean health-care workers gradually overcame those obstacles to their daily work. He told me about the excellent relations they had had with local residents and with the British.

Then, more confidentially, I asked him whether material interests were the main thing motivating the brigade members:

> We're human beings, and we have family needs. Who doesn't need money? Don't you? Everyone does. But from a professional point of view, no amount of money could pay you for this kind of mission. No amount of money could pay us for what we were able to do. We went on what was, in effect, a suicide mission. It's true it helped many

if not all of us solve some of our financial problems. But what if we hadn't returned home?

I could have gone to Qatar, and they would have paid me very well there. In fact, I was about to leave for Qatar, and yet I said: "No, I'm going here." I wanted to experience that moment in history. And I don't regret doing so.

People called us crazy. My wife told me I was crazy. The money wasn't going to make up for what we did. Never. The British earned $1,600 a day, plus expenses. And they asked us, "You came for free?" Yes, for free. We only received an allowance for expenses, not a salary, which Cuba refused. Whoever says he doesn't need the money is a liar. I love having money.

So now, you stop to think and you tell yourself: "Yes, it's true, I'm crazy." But you also think: "Well, what if the epidemic had ended up here in Cuba?"

In the end my family accepted what I did. They said, "It's amazing you accomplished that! How come you never told us anything?" Now they're proud of me. Now there's nothing but pride. This experience has marked my life.

What we did was an act of bravery

DR. ROTCEH RÍOS MOLINA

Captain Rotceh (Héctor spelled backward) is a specialist in internal medicine, commonly known in Cuba as a clinician. Only twenty-nine years old, he fast-tracked to become a specialist thanks to his academic achievements. He gets by pretty well in English. As soon as you meet him, you sense an air of confidence, a rare combination of aptitude and attitude. So it's not surprising he was asked to take on leadership and organizational responsibilities.

Among a hundred experienced doctors in Sierra Leone, Dr. Delgado chose him, almost from the first day, to direct very complex efforts. He was head of the Cuban medical team at the Waterloo ADRA treatment center and organized the work of thirty-six older co-workers—almost the same number of volunteers as the total serving in Guinea. He was one of the two Cuban doctors who entered the red zone the most times. But although he agreed right away to the proposal to go confront the Ebola hellhole, it took him a while before he let his loved ones know:

> With my family things were more difficult. There were already indications in the press that Cuba might send a medical brigade. Of course, they figured I might be chosen because of my medical specialty and because I was young. They were very distressed by that, and I had told them not to worry. Then I was called, and I accepted the assignment, but it took me a few days to talk to my family.
>
> I reported to the Central Medical Cooperation Unit, and we assembled there. Still, for four or five days I said nothing at home. I said I was attending a military training course. Finally, on Thursday or Friday of the week before departing, I had to sit my whole family down—my mother, my wife, everyone—and explain what the mission was. They understood, but they were worried something would happen to me.
>
> They still haven't gotten over the fright, so much so that my mother and my wife still haven't seen any of the photos I brought back. They can't look at them. Every time I play a video or show them the pictures I took, they begin to cry their eyes out. They just get upset, so I decided to file them in a computer folder and not show them. They'll

ask me specific details about the mission, which I answer, but they don't want me to say anything beyond that. They want to erase it, consider it over and done with.

What the center accomplished under Rotceh's leadership was first class. With the assistance of René Abeleira, an outstanding epidemiologist from Las Tunas, he organized preventive health measures at the hotel to ensure that none of the doctors under his responsibility or the Sierra Leonean medical workers would fall ill with malaria.

I'll tell you the number-one thing this experience gave me: the tremendous satisfaction of having saved so many lives. Some people might think that it was a small number, or that it was many. But I felt I did a lot for humanity and for those people who, when we came to care for them, had nothing. The biggest thing they had was us. And that recognition makes you feel good.

The second thing it gave me was a sense of professional competence, knowing you are an international doctor. People always talk, for example, about Harvard doctors, those who studied at Harvard or some other American university, or who work at a British clinic. But they have nothing on us. We're at the same level. Cuban doctors do wonders, and with our professional training we have no cause to envy any doctors in those countries.

I'm very competitive, in the sense of being the best possible professional. I always try to be a little better, to excel as a professional. I had the opportunity to spend time with doctors from other countries who were carrying out the same mission. And I saw that my fellow Cubans and I, without a doubt, were on the same level as them.

The other thing is something that has always been instilled in me: the spirit of solidarity, comradeship, brotherhood. I believe that's what allowed us all to return home safe and sound, except for the two we lost, one in Guinea and one from our team in Sierra Leone.

What we Cubans did there was an act of bravery. Nobody wanted to go there—they saw that if ten British doctors went in, two or three became ill. We were 165 and only one got sick. And his life was saved. I think that was a huge thing.

Guinea

Some history

It's a four-hour drive between Freetown and Conakry, the capital cities of Sierra Leone and Guinea. The two countries share ethnic groups and local languages, although outwardly they appear to be divided by the languages of their colonizers, English and French.

Traveling by air, however, is complicated because Air France has not had direct flights between the two cities since Ebola broke out. Instead, you have to make an almost twenty-hour trip via Casablanca, Morocco, with a long stopover there.

We arrived in Conakry exhausted. But the young Cuban ambassador, Maité Rivero Torres, and her husband, Daffne Ernesto Mirabal García, who came to welcome us, picked up our spirits with good news: the widow and son of Ahmed Sékou Touré, the founding president of independent Guinea, were waiting to see us right away. March 26, 2015, marked the thirty-first anniversary of Sékou Touré's death.

Since Fidel first visited Guinea in May 1972, the road to downtown Conakry has had a name that is as long as it's extravagant: the Fidel Castro Ruz Infinite Highway of History. On the way to the home of the Sékou Touré family, I reread the unusually brief speeches from Fidel's visit. Cuba and Guinea were two young revolutions with the same enemies: colonialism and neocolonialism. Sékou Touré, with characteristic African wisdom, had said at the time, "Guinea and Cuba are the two eyes of the same man." In his speeches Fidel would speak of a third country that had become a symbol of anti-imperialist struggle: Vietnam. Other leaders of the anticolonial movement had been awaiting Fidel's arrival in Conakry.

Fidel and Sékou Touré visited the regions of Kankan, Faranah, Labé, and Kindia. They drove to Kindia because Fidel felt that traveling by plane kept him too far from the people. "We like the human contact, because it's from the people that we draw our inspiration and encouragement, that we draw our lessons," Fidel said in a May 6, 1972, speech in Kindia. But he noted that perhaps his hosts wanted to show the best face of the country, not the extreme poverty of their countryside:

> Of course, we didn't come here to see rich villages. To see rich villages we would have planned a trip to Holland, Belgium, or Sweden, and the truth is we're not interested in those villages. If there's a village we're interested in, it's a Guinean village. And it won't surprise us to find poverty. What would really surprise us would be to find wealth in a Guinean village, because we know the imperialists exploit and plunder countries and leave no wealth, no prosperity. And we know that the merit of a revolution, the purpose of a revolution, and the cause of a revolution are precisely that injustice and poverty.

The affairs of the rich don't arouse our sympathy, they don't awaken our solidarity. Our solidarity and our sympathy are aroused by the man who fights, who works, who strives to better his condition, who struggles with poverty and carries it with dignity. We will never forget what compañero Sékou Touré said, that he preferred poverty with freedom over opulence with slavery. Of course, no slave will ever be opulent. And we free men will defeat backwardness and defeat poverty.

In Kankan, Faranah, and Labé there were Cuban doctors and nurses working as part of the Comprehensive Health Program. This medical cooperation program began in the early years of the revolution, and it hasn't stopped with the Ebola outbreak. To the contrary, a new brigade of thirty-seven men, members of the Henry Reeve Contingent, arrived to fight the epidemic in October 2014. Together with doctors from other African countries, they worked at the Ebola Treatment Unit in Coyah, the center that achieved the best results. The Guinean directors of that facility had studied medicine in Cuba.

We arrived at the home of this longtime friend of Cuba and were welcomed by his son, Mohamed Touré. The house was comfortable and spacious but simple. We sat on the back terrace, which afforded a view of the sea. The walls were covered with photos illustrating some of Africa's most recent history. One showed Fidel and Sékou Touré together. In another, Fidel and Amilcar Cabral were engaged in conversation. Mohamed told us:

> I want to express, first of all, my deep gratitude to the Cuban people and to their historic leader, commander Fidel Castro, the father of modern Cuba. I express this feeling on behalf of all of Africa, because the Cuban people have

always been at the side of the people of Africa in their struggles for liberation and human dignity. The spirit of the Cuban Revolution is a universal one.

Hadja Andrée Touré, widow of the great founding leader, arrived while her son was speaking. A serene, sweet elderly woman, she discreetly sat on a couch far from us so as not to interrupt. We met with her a few minutes later. We talked about Fidel's first visit. "Thank you so much for coming all the way here," she said, as if it was she who was honored and not us.

> You know that Fidel Castro is a great friend of Guinea. Fidel's visit brought us much closer. Our people gave him a fitting welcome, that is, the way you welcome a great man who comes from a great country. Cuba has helped us a lot, and Guineans cannot forget that.
>
> During his visit he acted as though he was just another Guinean. He visited the interior of the country and, as the unassuming man that he is, would connect with the people all the time. There's a photo where he is sitting on a staircase next to people, talking with the young women of the protocol staff. He is a very humble man (she smiles at the memory). When he arrived, as a security measure, President Sékou Touré gave him his bed; he slept in the president's room.

Oscar Oramas, then Cuban ambassador to Guinea, writes in his interesting, as yet unpublished memoirs that Sékou Touré told the commander-in-chief, "Well, Fidel, I brought you here because this is my house and from now on it's yours—this is where you'll stay. One of the traditions of my people is that you offer your own home and bed to someone you consider your best friend."

It was inevitable that we would talk about the Cuban doctors involved in the fight against Ebola. Mohamed was categorical:

> Cuba has always been here, in Africa, in Guinea. It has trained thousands and thousands of Guinean cadres, hundreds of Guinean doctors who, had they been efficiently organized, would have been able to stop Ebola. What Cuba is doing now is continuing a tradition.
>
> We will never be grateful enough to the Cuban people. I've given some examples of Cuba's cooperation, but nothing surpasses its contribution to our independence. Cuban soldiers have died on the battlefield to liberate Africa. So the response to Ebola, for us, is one more step in the long tradition of cooperation between the Cuban people and the people of Africa.

Hadja Andre Touré reiterated her son's words:

> Cuba has always been close to us. It helped us train doctors. The best doctors in Guinea were trained in Cuba. That Cuba should come to assist us again is no surprise. I want to thank the Cuban people once again for all the help they have offered us over all these years.

In Guinea I realized that if I wanted to write about the internationalist feat of the Cuban doctors in the fight against Ebola, I would have to give some background on Cuba's half-century of actions in solidarity with Africa. In each of our discussions with Guinean doctors, officials, or ministers, the backdrop was the long relationship between the countries on the African continent and the small Caribbean island.

Perhaps this was because the Guinean directors of the

Ebola Treatment Unit in Coyah had graduated from Cuban universities. Or because the leaders of the National Coordination Center for the Fight Against Ebola had also done so. Or perhaps because, as one Guinean told me, seemingly formal coincidences sometimes reveal the existence of deeper historical processes. That's the view of intellectual and diplomat Elhadj Bangaly Dabo, who studied in Cuba in 1961, married a Cuban woman, and translated for Fidel to the Mandingo language during his first visit to Kankan. Dabo explained:

> There are similarities between the history of Cuba and that of Guinea. In the second half of the nineteenth century, Cuba was in the midst of its independence struggle, led by great military and political figures. In Guinea during the same period, Samory Touré was fighting the French.
>
> In 1953 the attack on the Moncada barracks took place in Cuba, and here, the seventy-two-day truckers' strike. For seventy-two days women stopped selling their products, which was their livelihood. The men didn't go to work and weren't paid.
>
> Guinea won its freedom in late 1958 and Cuba in early 1959. I believe the first time Fidel and Sékou Touré met was in Algiers in 1959.
>
> In addition, [in September 1960] when the Americans refused to let Fidel stay in their luxury hotels, the New York neighborhood of Harlem extended their hospitality to him, and Sékou Touré was the first head of state to visit him there. He was also the first African head of state to visit Cuba, on October 14, 1960. A mercenary invasion was launched against Cuba [at Playa Girón] in 1961, and one was launched against Conakry in 1970. Fidel's first visit to Africa was to Guinea.

These were not mere bilateral ties, nor were they pure coincidences. Cairo under Gamal Abdel Nasser, Kwame Nkrumah's Accra, Algiers under Houari Boumediene, and the Conakry of Sékou Touré were the capitals where the great anticolonial leaders of Africa met and gathered. But as Mohamed Touré told me, "If we're going to talk about the great historic leaders of Africa, we have to start with Fidel Castro Ruz, who for us is an African, a Cuban, a world figure, a hero of Africa's liberation struggle." Both Cuba and Guinea gave active support to the liberation of the continent.

President Alpha Condé recalled an episode that was part of this close relationship: "After the war broke out in Angola and South Africa intervened, there was a meeting in Conakry between Presidents Castro, Sékou Touré, and Agostinho Neto, where it was agreed that Cuban troops traveling to Angola would make a stopover in Conakry."

Alhousseine Makanera Kaké, Guinea's minister of communications, began his meeting with the Cuban press team saying, "Guineans know Cubans well," and he added, "particularly in my case, because I'm from Boké." He was referring to the fact that in the late 1960s and early '70s, some Cuban soldiers and doctors were based in the town of Boké, near Guinea's border with the small country of Guinea-Bissau. They were serving as instructors and military doctors with the African Party for the Independence of Guinea and Cape Verde (PAIGC), led by the great Amilcar Cabral, which was conducting the struggle against Portuguese colonial rule.

On my return to Cuba I took advantage of my mandatory quarantine period to read the enjoyable and well-documented history of Cuba's relations with Africa by Italian-American writer Piero Gleijeses, *Conflicting Missions: Havana, Washington, and Africa, 1959–1976.* The quarantine was required of all travelers returning from that region, an extreme measure Cuba took to prevent the enemy's prediction from being fulfilled.

The ties between Guinea and Cuba were strengthened when, after a decisive meeting in 1965 between Cabral and Che Guevara in Conakry, Cabral visited Cuba and spoke with Fidel. Cuba's decision to support the liberation movement in Guinea-Bissau and Cape Verde, whose headquarters was in Conakry, brought the two governments closer.

From Gleijeses's written history, I was lucky enough to come directly in contact with living history. I met Víctor Dreke at an October 2015 historians conference in Havana, where he was participating not as a historian but as a maker of history. He agreed to an interview. He is a lively, clear-minded seventy-eight-year-old, but his revolutionary activity began when he was fifteen. I will highlight just some of Dreke's best-known experiences working with the African independence movements. These were his role as second in command under Che of the Cuban guerrillas in the Congo in 1965, and then as head of the Cuban instructors in Amilcar Cabral's guerrilla force in Guinea-Bissau:

> I arrived in Conakry in 1966 as head of the Cuban military mission in Guinea-Conakry and Guinea-Bissau, which as you know share a border. Nobody knows where one country begins and the other ends, although they say a river divides them. The economic situation of the population was terrible.
>
> The French had left Guinea-Conakry after Sékou told them "No," which should not be forgotten by history.[1]

1. In face of the anticolonial struggles sweeping Africa, the Charles de Gaulle government in Paris held a referendum on a new French constitution in September 1958. Those voting in the French colonies in sub-

They took everything with them, down to the nails, as we say. They tore down and took away the traffic lights. The Donka Hospital, the only one at the time, was closed. When we arrived, one of the things we did was to assign a Cuban doctor to that hospital, which was the only one in the capital. The only hospital the Guinea-Bissau and Cape Verde liberation movement had was in Boké. It's important to know that the first internationalist medical assistance Guinea-Bissau received was provided by Cuban military doctors, who were part of the guerilla force. They not only cared for our combatants and those from Guinea-Bissau, but for the local population including residents of Boké, Guinea-Conakry. In addition, the first nurses trained for Guinea-Bissau were trained at the Boké hospital, by the late Dr. Noroña, very well-known there; Dr. Castillo; and several other compañeros, including Castell, a laboratory technician. They trained the first group of health-care workers.

The arrival of Cuban doctors and guerrillas was welcomed by the Guinea-Bissau liberation forces. The presence of Cuban medical personnel contributed to the psychological well-being of the combatants—they knew they wouldn't die just because they were wounded or contracted a curable illness.

Saharan Africa had the choice of either approving the new constitution and maintaining colonial status under one of various forms, or, if they rejected the constitution, of gaining independence. De Gaulle threatened that the latter choice would lead to immediate loss of French economic "aid" and withdrawal of French administrative and technical personnel. The independence movement in Guinea, whose central leader was Ahmed Sékou Touré, successfully campaigned for a "No" vote. Guinea became independent in October 1958, with Sékou Touré as its first president.

In addition to the doctors, there were Cuban military instructors in the jungle of the small Portuguese colony, as Gleijeses writes in *Conflicting Missions*:

> By April 1967 there were almost sixty Cubans in Guinea-Bissau, including several who had been in Zaire [Congo] with Che Guevara. Dreke himself spent half his time in Conakry and half at the front. He was in Conakry when, in October 1967, Guevara was killed in Bolivia. . . . Between 1966 and 1974 there were, on average, fifteen to twenty Cuban doctors and nurses in Guinea-Bissau and Boké. (pp. 191, 202)

Of course, Cuban collaboration extended to other fields:

> The growth in Cuban aid was also evident in the increasing numbers of Africans studying there [in Cuba]. The first foreign scholarship students in Castro's Cuba were from Guinea in 1961. Over the next fifteen years, small numbers of Africans continued to arrive in Cuba. In 1969, for example, there were 65 from the Congo, 29 from Guinea, and 36 from Guinea-Bissau. The numbers increased dramatically when, in 1972–1974, Guinea sent 400 university students to Havana. (Gleijeses, p. 228)

Dr. Sékou Keita, deputy director of the Ebola Treatment Unit in Coyah, was one of those four hundred young people who came to the island with a backpack full of dreams:

> I studied in Cuba from 1972 to 1979. Cuba helped me build my life, not only thanks to the technical knowledge I received. That helped me, of course, to get to where I am, because everyone respects me for what I learned, for the lives I've saved. I'm a gynecologist—I did the internship

program where the final year is devoted to a specialty. And here I'm the only gynecologist for a population of 179,000.

The revolutionary history of Cuba is amazing—first the insurrectional struggle, followed by the broader struggle of the people, from which hundreds of outstanding individuals emerged. The greatest strength and achievement of a revolution, contrary to what is commonly assumed, lies in its ability to transform the masses into groups of individuals that play a leading role in history.

Africa has been the arena for many extraordinary individual actions by Cubans. For one thing, three of the five Cuban heroes, who spent as many as sixteen years locked up in US prisons, earlier fought as soldiers in Angola against the invasions by South African and Zairean forces at two key moments in that conflict. They are René González Sehwerert (1977–79), Fernando González Llort (1987–89), and Gerardo Hernández Nordelo (1989–90). The subsequent story of resistance by these men, who refused to give up in face of a long and unjust imprisonment under harsh conditions, had a precedent in Africa.[2]

Orlando Cardoso Villavicencio, a young Cuban lieutenant, was wounded in combat and taken prisoner by Somali forces in Ethiopia. He was held in solitary confinement in

2. Gerardo Hernández, Ramón Labañino, Antonio Guerrero, Fernando González and René González—known in Cuba as the Five Heroes and around the world as the Cuban Five—were arrested in Florida in 1998 and framed up by Washington on "conspiracy" and other charges. They had been reporting to the Cuban government on counterrevolutionary groups in the US planning terrorist attacks against Cuba. They spent up to sixteen years in US prisons, the last three being released in 2014. For more on the participation by Hernández, Fernando González, and René González in Cuba's mission in Angola, see *Cuba and Angola: Fighting for Africa's Freedom and Our Own*, published by Pathfinder Press.

his captors' dungeons for almost eleven years. Years passed before he found out Cuba knew of his existence and had been negotiating his release, a fact that makes his resistance even more heroic.

Reading Gleijeses, I learned of another individual story, that of then-captain Pedro Rodríguez Peralta, an internationalist instructor in southern Guinea-Bissau who in 1969 was wounded and captured by Portuguese paratroopers. As Víctor Dreke, his former commanding officer, told me:

> I wasn't there when he was captured. He was initially with me and then stayed on the southern front. He violated some orders. Pedrito, who was a very brave compañero, had been advised not to go out alone. The Portuguese had been trying to capture Cubans for some time. But it must also be said that Pedro spent five years in prison and comported himself the way he was supposed to, always defending Cuba. That's what happened.

Rodríguez Peralta, following what had been agreed to with Amilcar Cabral, denied having any official relationship with his country and was sentenced to ten years. An unanticipated event cut short his time in prison:

> On April 25, 1974, war-weary Portuguese officers overthrew the dictatorship and brought their country's imperial folly to an end. On September 10, Portugal recognized the Republic of Guinea-Bissau. That same day, Rodríguez Peralta's name first appeared in the Cuban press, when *Granma* mentioned, out of the blue, that Lisbon had announced that he would soon be freed. (Another article, six days later, mentioned that he had been captured in 1969 in Guinea-Bissau.)
>
> Rodríguez Peralta returned to Cuba on September 16,

1974. In a front-page three-column article, *Granma* described his arrival at the airport where Fidel Castro and top Cuban officials were waiting for him; it described Rodríguez Peralta's suffering at the hands of his captors, but it said not one word about Cuba's aid to the PAIGC. (Gleijeses, p. 211)

I tried to imagine Conakry in those years of revolutionary upsurge. I read Oscar Oramas's memoirs in one sitting and with a little envy. He was one of the last people to see Amilcar Cabral alive, and one of the first to see him shot down in the streets of the Guinean capital. I was also riveted by the anecdotes and observations of Víctor Dreke, who fought at the side of Che in the Congo and Amilcar in Guinea-Bissau, leaders who themselves worked with important figures of that time. Outstanding champions of the anticolonial struggle lived in or visited Conakry in those days: Sékou Touré, Amilcar Cabral, Kwame Nkrumah of Ghana, Julius Nyerere of Tanzania, Kenneth Kaunda of Zambia, and Djibo Bakary of Niger, among others. So did many young Cubans, heroes whose names barely appear in history books.

"What motivated them?" Gleijeses asks in his book. Ulises Estrada, one of the Cuban combatants, replies, "We dreamed of revolution. We wanted to be part of it."

Gleijeses adds, "The volunteers received no public praise in Cuba. . . . They won no medals or material rewards." (p. 204)

Dr. Ana Morales Valera met Dreke in 1986 in post-independence Guinea-Bissau, when she was working as head of the Cuban medical mission; she has been his steadfast companion ever since. During those years she was given and carried out the assignment of establishing the first medical school in sub-Saharan Africa. Joining my discussion

with Dreke, she told me they were putting together the
biographies of the hundred-thirty men who were in Che's
guerrilla force in the Congo. Young, modest revolutionaries—their average age was twenty-four—who continued to
be modest and revolutionary. For twenty years they kept the
secret of their participation, and their names are not well-
known. Some don't even remember their nom de guerre.

Incidentally, several of the Cuban doctors who volunteered to combat Ebola had previously served in Angola
during the war. For example, in Monrovia, Dr. Gerardo
Rodríguez Ricardo of Holguín, a sixty-one-year-old epidemiologist and specialist in infectious diseases, recalled
his Angola days:

> I also had the opportunity to witness the courage of the
> Cubans there. There were wounded combatants who,
> when I tended to them, simply told me, "Patch me up, I'm
> going back to the front."
>
> I'd reply, "No, we've brought you here in an ambu-
> lance"—and they'd say, "No, no, I'm going. Just put some
> antiseptic on it so I can go back."
>
> I had that opportunity, seeing firsthand the courage
> of the Cuban volunteers. That experience stayed with me.
> I wanted to write a book like you—I have some notes
> at home. I wanted to write some things about Angola
> because it marked me for life. When Operation Tribute
> arrived in Cuba—the return of the remains of the fallen
> combatants—I stayed home all day crying. I'm telling you
> the truth.

Cuba's solidarity, however, was not limited to liberation
movements and progressive governments. It's hard to find
an African country where there are no graduates of Cuban universities, and few African states have not received

humanitarian assistance from our small Caribbean island. One of the hotels that hosted Cuban doctors and nurses in Freetown has an unusual name: "Compañero," just like that, in Spanish. Its owner, of course, studied in Cuba. The wall along the entrance ramp has a mural depicting Fidel at two different periods in his life—in one image he's standing next to the current president of Sierra Leone, and in the other, next to the hotel owner, naturally. The two countries' flags are also painted on the wall. In Africa, affinity with Cuba or with men such as Fidel or Che does not necessarily mean ideological affinity.

In Freetown, Tony Pubillones, the chargé d'affaires, went with us to visit opposition leader Sulaiman Banja Tejan-Sie, secretary general of the People's Party. A photo of Queen Elizabeth II of the United Kingdom sat on his desk, yet he said with conviction, "Fidel Castro represents our aspirations, not only those of Cuba. The government and the opposition in Sierra Leone speak with one voice when it comes to Cuba."

Fidel's October 2, 2014, article on the health workers who left to fight Ebola in Africa, "Heroes of our time," began, not coincidentally, with an account of the heroism of the Cubans in Angola. Internationalism is an expression of revolutionary humanism. As Fidel wrote, "The decisive victory of 1959—this we can state without a hint of chauvinism—became an example of what a small nation, while fighting for itself, can also do for others."

Objections

The rapid arrival of Cuban doctors in Guinea surprised the World Health Organization and local institutions. They weren't prepared to take on such a large number of volunteers, and our doctors were initially greeted with some doubts. A prestigious NGO, citing irrelevant arguments, put obstacles in the way of training and certifying our volunteers. Dr. Graciliano Díaz told us, "At first it was difficult to start working on Ebola. We're not sure why, but it seems those who opposed us thought we had come to compete with them. The truth is we had no such desire. We came to fight Ebola, which in fact had cost many of them their lives."

Two objections were put forward. First, that the Cubans for the most part didn't speak French. Second, that they had never worked with Ebola patients before. The second objection was ridiculous. Most of the doctors and nurses—foreign and local—who worked in the Ebola Treatment Units had never done so before either. There's always a first time, and given the kind of disease we were faced with, that was the case for almost everyone involved.

Our personnel, however, came armed with solid theoretical and practical training, and enough experience and professional expertise to quickly learn what was necessary. President Condé settled the dispute. During an interview he told us:

> One problem we had was the contradictions. When the Cuban doctors arrived, for example, there were people who said: Cuba has no experience with Ebola, but we know the best doctors in Africa are the Cubans. I was in Venezuela and visited the grassroots communities—the doctors and dentists were Cuban. It's the same in Brazil. And in 1960 Guinea was one of the first countries in Africa to establish relations with Cuba; since then we've had Cuban doctors. When the Russian laboratory arrived, some said it wasn't operational, but when we inspected it, we saw it was as operational as the rest.

The different organizations continued to react the way they were used to reacting in past situations. But Ebola was something very different. Everyone had to agree to work together. We had a lot of trouble achieving real coordination.

People also said, "The Cubans don't speak French." But others replied that many Guineans had been trained in Cuba. If the Cubans worked with those Guineans, there would be no language barriers. So everything that was raised as an obstacle was in fact not a problem. Cuban doctors are doing a very good job.

Dr. Sakoba Keita, national coordinator in Guinea of the fight against Ebola, had been trained in Cuba. He said the following about these initial objections:

I was part of many of these discussions, and those who talked to me about Cuba forgot I was trained by Cubans. So I would ask, "Do you have confidence in me?"

"There's no problem with you."

"Then there's no problem with Cuba, because I spent seven years in Cuba to acquire the knowledge I have."

In Coyah, where the brigade is working, there are two Guinean doctors who trained with me in Cuba. And that's why those doctors have such good results. It's thanks to the Cuban-trained team of Guineans and the brigade that has come here.

At first there were people who said the Cubans couldn't work in an Ebola Treatment Unit. Two days before the opening of the center, I was told I'd have to take responsibility if there were any problem. I answered, "If any problem arises because of a Cuban or a Guinean trained in Cuba, I'll resign from my post."

Now everyone knows this is our best center. The first

place that foreigners coming to Guinea visit is Coyah—to see the Cuban brigade and the team there. And I'm very happy about that, because what I said has been accomplished in practice.

The youngest volunteers took on the risk as a professional challenge, as scientists eager to deepen their experience. Dr. Osvaldo Miranda Gómez, thirty-eight, understood this on a personal level as a Cuban scientist:

> There was also the language challenge. I don't know much French; others do. But we had to prove we could do it. Because in the end, who knew about Ebola? No one. What was in the books—and who writes the books? People. Who are Doctors Without Borders? People. Doctors just like us. They're not born with the knowledge.
>
> It's a critical combination of events, a political problem. From a medical point of view, once you begin to study epidemiology, you dream of being part of an action like this. An epidemiologist aspires to be on the scene, in the middle of a big epidemic.

How it began

Dr. Carlos Castro Baras, head of the brigade in Guinea, told us how it all began:

> When we arrived in Conakry, we confronted the fact that we were missing phase three of the training. We had completed the second phase with instructors from the World Health Organization at a transit center in the Guinean town of Forécariah, but we hadn't done phase three, which

was with patients. After a lot of effort we arranged for two of our colleagues, a doctor and a nurse, to train with Doctors Without Borders at the Donka Hospital in Conakry. Only two, which was not enough. We kept looking for options and managed to get another six—three doctors and three nurses—to train in Kérouané, in the region called Forested Guinea [in the southeast]. They were the only ones who had done training with patients when we went to Coyah.

Construction had begun on the center in October. It officially opened December 19, but when we moved in on the 27th it still wasn't operational. We began to arrange things in the center ourselves, setting up furniture, assembling beds, installing the equipment. We wanted to begin work on December 31, to mark the anniversary of the revolution. At 2:00 p.m. on December 31, the first group, headed by Dr. Yoel Fleites, started work, and at exactly 5:02 p.m. the first patient came in, a confirmed case.

We were all afraid at the beginning—afraid when we suited up, afraid when we entered the red zone, afraid when we touched anything, when we walked. We had all the symptoms of psychological terror. So for the first few nights we talked a lot with the volunteers. The hygienists they had sent us had no previous training, meaning we had to learn and teach at the same time. We had to find a balance to make sure that each group had medical personnel from Guinea and other African Union countries. This helped us establish a rapport with the Guineans and other Africans.

We had to overcome the psychological barriers quickly. Because of the center's geographical location near the epicenter of the epidemic, we received many patients from districts surrounding Conakry. We had to act swiftly so the center didn't collapse due to the sheer number of patients arriving. It was a really beautiful experience.

The Coyah Treatment Unit

The Coyah Ebola Treatment Unit was about 35 miles from Conakry. Coyah is a district with a small, dusty town of the same name. Cubans lived and worked in the nearby town of Wonkifong. Every day they traveled in both directions along a paved stretch of highway. For several days we traveled this route with the doctors and nurses of each shift.

The brigade was divided into four teams that rotated between morning, afternoon, and evening shifts. The shifts worked twenty-four hours a day, seven days a week. Each team included doctors and nurses from Guinea and other African countries. There was also a team made up solely of African Union health workers.

To get to the small La Hacienda Hotel, where the Cubans stayed, you had to get off the highway and follow a dirt road. The center, at the other end of the daily run, was also deep in the countryside. There was no other place for the Cuban brigade to go: they were either at the center or in the hotel, a pleasant facility with small cone-shaped cabins surrounded by a long wall around the perimeter. There was electricity twelve hours a day, not always the same hours. The center, however, was a field hospital that met all the requirements.

Temperatures in Guinea at this time of year can reach 50 degrees Celsius (122 degrees Fahrenheit). The protective suit you had to wear to enter the hospital's red zone was nearly hermetically sealed and the extra heat from wearing it induced fatigue.

Despite all this, the Cubans made their presence felt when they arrived with their characteristic exuberance, their jokes and boisterous greetings. There was no time to yearn for home—the constant and sometimes tense work, as well as the good spirits, cut short any hint of homesickness. Dr. Castro Baras had succeeded in drawing his thirty-seven men together as a cohesive group.

Before entering the center, they would wash their hands in a chlorine solution; the soles of their shoes were fumigated. The encounter with the patients had a big impact. People arrived at the Coyah center from all regions around the capital. The epicenter of the epidemic had migrated to this area, and the government wanted to prevent it from taking hold in the country's most populous city.

Around 70 percent of those arriving were positive for Ebola. Many had been referred with a confirmed diagnosis. This, as well as the fact that most were admitted on the sixth or seventh day after exposure, raised the fatality rate, which was 52.3 percent. Actually, thanks to the discipline and professionalism of the Cubans and other health workers at the center, this rate was lower than the average for the rest of the country, which stood at 66.5 percent.

It was difficult, however, for local residents, a majority of them illiterate, who neither read nor listened to public announcements about the disease, to readily welcome what to them was a mysterious place, inhabited by foreigners dressed as "astronauts." Some of the sick would hide, or they didn't recognize the symptoms.

This is what we were told by Fofana, a young woman who—together with her child, who was three or four years old—contracted Ebola and whose life was saved in this hospital. When asked, she didn't know her own age but simply said she had four children. Her mother-in-law had fallen ill earlier but didn't want to be admitted, and she died. Fofana contracted the virus when she washed the body for the funeral ceremony. She then passed it on to her young daughter. "This place used to scare people," Fofana said. Her words were translated by a health counselor who spoke her language and who was trying to convince her to become an activist for the center. "But here I discovered that everything that was being said outside was a lie. I always received good food and treatment. I'm very grateful, very happy, because we were both cured."

That morning was especially beautiful, because six Ebola patients were discharged. The government had just declared a heightened state of emergency in the regions surrounding the capital, and further mandatory measures were probably coming. But the Cuban brigade had come here in order to save lives.

After the shift handover, Dr. Yoel Fleites, responsible for the incoming team, gave out the assignments and designated those who were going into the red zone today: Dr. Ivo Zúñiga, the youngest of the group, who was just twenty-eight, and Rogelio Labrador and Reinaldo Expósito, the nurses.

Explaining his reasons for coming to Guinea, Dr. Zúñiga told me:

> I came with the backing of my family. At first they didn't want me to come, but later they gave me their support. I got them to understand that as a doctor I had to see this disease up close, touch it with my hands. We had seen it in books, I knew about it from brief articles, but not in the way you experience it here. I volunteered because I wanted to learn firsthand.

The most delicate task, and the one that determined the success or failure of the sanitary efforts, was the long, meticulous process in which each doctor and nurse, assisted by co-workers, prepared to enter the red zone, whether in the hospital or the community. The suit, made of a synthetic waterproof material, covered the whole body except the face, which was protected by special goggles and a surgical mask. The Cuban health workers would then seal the area around the face with surgical tape.

They wore two pairs of rubber gloves. They opened a hole in the sleeve of the suit with a sharp object, at hand level, through which they introduced their thumbs. That way, the sleeve wouldn't slide back. Someone wrote on their chest the first or last name of the doctor or nurse and their specialty, so the patient could identify him. Smiling eyes looked at us from behind the safety glasses.

The undressing ritual was more complex and dangerous, because the suit was already contaminated and any skin contact with the outside surface could produce the unwanted contagion. With the guidance of a colleague supervising each step as the health worker undressed, and with a decontamination worker spraying the used suit with a chlorine solution, the doctors and nurses began the process of removing each piece of their clothing. At the end, everything was incinerated.

Three plastic fences separated the sick patients from the workers. From the green zone we could observe almost all the activity of the group inside. They administered medication, inserted IVs, and if necessary bathed the patient. Both doctors and nurses performed similar tasks; here there were no presumed hierarchies. Food, clothing, and any medication requested by the doctor or the patient were dropped through a wooden chute. All objects passed to the other side were subsequently incinerated.

From our observation point, we saw a girl with frightened eyes. We were informed she was an orphan being cared for by a patient who had been cured and was now immune to this strain. An hour later the "astronauts" returned to the green zone, after going through the meticulous, delicate procedure in which they were undressed and disinfected. They arrived sweaty, exhausted by the effort, but still joking around.

Each shift seemed to go quickly—the workload left no room for waiting around. Everyone knew the epidemic remained a serious threat in the country, and nobody asked when they would return home.

By May 2015 the Coyah ETU had admitted 350 patients, 244 of them confirmed Ebola cases. Of the overall total, 207 were released alive, 111 of whom had been infected.

Coyah was a model for the country—it achieved the best results. Led by Guineans and supported by medical personnel from Cuba and the African Union, it became the center of the fight against Ebola in Guinea.

Religious and ethnic questions

One Friday during my stay in Conakry, I asked the authorities for a special permit to observe and take photos of the ceremony in the Grand Mosque. The largest mosque in West Africa, it was built during the government of President Ahmed Sékou Touré and can accommodate 12,500 people at any given time. If the attendance is larger, the faithful sit and pray in the outer esplanade, where the imam's sermon is amplified with loudspeakers. Women do not enter the mosque but pray outside.

Every Friday at 1:00 p.m., Muslims go to the nearest mosque and take part in the ritual inside or outside. Sometimes, if the mosque is small, surrounding streets are closed off. Every Friday President Alpha Condé attends a different mosque, which may be big or small, rich or poor. He goes to share the traditional ritual with the faithful, as well as to show support for the imam and receive his support. Every Friday men wear their elegant, long robes. I took many pictures that day, but the one that became popular among our epidemiologists was a photo of four bodies placed in the center of a large room where the imam rested before beginning his ritual. Two were in closed coffins and two were shrouded in mats of wood and cloth. As a special guest, I was invited to share the imam's room with him. I spent a few seconds there, some distance from the bodies, and took the photo—a habit that can become an obsession.

Interethnic tensions in Africa are well-known. The colonial powers cut up the continent like a cake, each one vying to grab the biggest, most appetizing, or simply most available slice of "nature" (read: natural resources). In the process, their borders divided many indigenous cultures, languages, and traditions. For the colonialists it was more important to keep a gold, diamond, or other mine intact than a culture.

This also made domination easier. The colonialists pitted ethnic groups against each other, handing out petty privileges or benefits, or stirring up conflicts based on warring traditions or ethnic lineages. The independent "national" states were finally constituted on the basis of those schizophrenic partitions, perpetuating the ethnic conflicts. Cuban international relations scholars David González López and Clara Pulido Escandell have noted:

> Most African political parties have been institutions of a combined nature—nominally "modern" but, more often than not, ethnically based. To the extent these politi-

cal parties were "modern" institutions with a "traditional" ethnic base (and often their leaders, or their associates or trusted men, were traditional chiefs), newly independent governments maintained the economic and political alliances previously forged with ethnic groups during the colonial period. They often used governmental forms similar to those the colonial power had created. (*Cuadernos África–América Latina*, no. 27–28, 1997)

On the other hand, as ethnologist Rodolfo Stavenhagen writes in his book *Ethnic Conflicts and the Nation-State*:

Economic factors play a crucial role in the generation of ethnic conflicts. When regional and social disparities in the distribution of economic resources also reflect differences between identified ethnic groups, then conflicts over social and economic issues readily turn into ethnic conflicts. (p. 294)

The same Friday that I visited the Grand Mosque in Conakry, we met with Koutoubou Moustapha Sano, Guinea's minister for international cooperation, who had made it possible for me to see the religious site. After a long conversation about Cuba's cooperation and his government's strategy in the fight against Ebola, I asked him about the issue of ethnic conflicts. With the following quotations from his remarks, I don't pretend to exhaust such a complex subject. But I think it's important for the reader to appreciate the social context in which the epidemic unfolded.

The minister's response surprised me. While different groups remain able to mobilize along ethnic lines and maintain their identity, they have started to intermix within families:

Ethnic conflicts here don't have a religious connotation. The majority of the population, 90 percent, is Muslim. Christians are a minority. But ethnic conflicts translate into political conflicts. Frequently, politicians use ethnic conflicts for their own purposes, but there is no actual conflict because the ethnic groups are intermixed. My father is Malinke, my mother is from the region of Middle Guinea and is Fulani, or Peul. My wife is Fulani, my sister's husband is Fulani, my nephew and my nieces are also Fulani.

I think what politicians do is simply manipulate the ethnic factor: Malinke against Fulani, Fulani against Soussou, Soussou against Malinke. But it doesn't last long—it's short-lived. Fortunately we've never had a civil war. We haven't had one because there are four major ethnic groups, and none is large enough to be an absolute majority. Maybe one group is a majority in relation to another, but not for all of Guinea.

We have the Fulani, the Soussou, the Malinke, and the Kpelle peoples. If there is a conflict between two of them, and they each seek out the others, whoever manages to win over the other two wins the conflict. Therefore, if three groups are in agreement, the fourth has to accept. On the other hand, during the election campaign many slogans are put forward, there is a lot of talk, but in the end none of it is real.

For example, if I'm with the government party, my wife may be with the opposition because she is Fulani. We talk, and she says, "Well, it's you and us." And I say, "Well, but we won," and she has to accept it. There are clashes for a few days, at most a week, but then it's over. The opposition leader, for example, is my brother-in-law. Therefore I see him, we greet each other, I can go to his house, and he can come to mine. But during the election campaign he doesn't know me and I don't know him. We're in campaign mode. If he wins, good.

We also have to accept the fact that sometimes there are tensions among the youth. They become agitated and get involved in acts of violence. But that doesn't last, because they end up seeing each other in their own homes. My sister's husband is Fulani and her children are Fulani-Malinke. I have a brother whose wife is Soussou and his children are a mixture. But politics is politics.

Diamond Plaza

Just as we were about to leave Conakry, we visited what is known as Plaza Diamant (Diamond Plaza), an extraordinary urban oasis, hard to believe but very real. It's almost entirely walled off, protected by advanced security systems. This is a residential area with luxury apartments and homes for millionaires, expensive restaurants and shops. Construction remains in full swing.

Walking into the lobby of the complex, we saw a scale model of the seventeen-hectare [forty-two-acre] project. Near the reception desk are surveillance TV screens scanning every corner, and the security staff monitoring the images. We identified ourselves and were accompanied by a beautiful, discreet guide/saleswoman.

Most of the residences were still empty. I thought to myself that the real estate business backing this investment must have been hurt by the epidemic. Still, I felt uncomfortable. It wasn't even remotely likely I would ever have the money to afford it (and that's also true of most Guineans I knew or saw in the capital, regardless of ethnic background), but even if I did, there's no way I'd be able to live inside this bubble.

There is a huge common swimming pool at the entrance of this small "city," but that doesn't prevent any home from having its own pool if the buyer so requests. We entered a display unit, furnished according to the typical mediocre taste of the well-heeled, and went through it room by room. The guide told us the price tag: $1.5 million. In the scale model, the "futuristic" city appeared surrounded by green areas. In reality those areas don't exist. It's all stalls, houses, shacks, and hundreds of street vendors that surround this strange paradise, admission to which is not gained by good behavior. The displaced residents who walked by the project seemed proud of its odd beauty.

The Cuban ambassador's residence, on the other hand, is quite a distance from Diamond Plaza, in a centrally located area near the shore. It's an elegant but aging house whose architectural style evokes a vaguely African spirit. There are ten or twelve identical houses in the vicinity, originally designed for a Pan-African summit that never took place. A few meters from the residence, a wooden bridge juts out over the water to a house on stilts, also made of wood. The place appears very precarious and about to collapse, but it's solidly built. This is the Obama Restaurant, and inside there's a portrait of the First Lady of the United States. I suppose the epidemic kept many diners from coming. But one night I observed from afar a large group of people having a noisy party there. A curious neighbor said they were US diplomats.

The day is divided between high tide and low tide, and depending on these flows the shoreline approaches or recedes, exposing a dirty, muddy terrain littered with the most unexpected urban debris. The bridge and the restaurant do not stand over water all day.

A little further down is a pier with colorful boats that

come and go from the small inhabited sea islands. During high tide they dock at the pier. During low tide they wait out at sea, while a small army of persistent vendors, some knee-deep or waist-deep in water, seek out passengers while carrying all kinds of goods for sale on their shoulders and heads. At the dock, dozens of boats remain stuck in the mud for as long as the low tide lasts.

Globalization dictates its brands. One of the boats is named *Real Madrid*. On the prow, the soccer-loving owner painted two letters and a number: CR7.[3]

---

3. A nickname for Cristiano Ronaldo, number 7 on the Real Madrid soccer team.

The men III

Five long, intense months

DR. CARLOS MANUEL CASTRO BARAS

Col. Castro Baras's incisive gaze invites candid conversation. Despite his brusque frankness and the occasionally ironic tone of his words, he is liked by his subordinates. He is known for listening to everyone, whatever problem they may have, and demonstrates two rarely combined virtues: flexibility and ability to command. From his first words, you see both the leader and the potential friend.

A military doctor (though he graduated from medical school as a civilian), he had previously served in the Angolan war as a twenty-eight-year-old lieutenant. That was the rank conferred on university students in Cuba after graduation. Although entrance to a higher education institution exempted them from military service, they received military training as part of their university studies. As he told me:

> Angola was my first major experience, serving as head of medical services in a tank brigade, first in the north and

then in Huambo. I was still very inexperienced and im-
mature. I didn't have the honor of taking part in combat,
but I did care for many who were wounded in action by
mine explosions and accidents. I spent twenty-six months
in Angola. I was promoted to captain there and admitted
as a party member.

After specializing in health administration, Dr. Castro
took on various responsibilities, including as director of
a sanitarium and as deputy director and director of two
military hospitals in Havana. But his responsibility as head
of the medical brigade in Guinea was the most challenging, he said. "Five long, intense months are leaving their
mark on me," he wrote in some personal notes. When we
met, he explained:

> In this war the enemy is invisible. It's there, but you don't
> know where. Here you can die under any circumstances.
> The disease has many modes of transmission, many safety
> risks, and the slightest error can cost you your life. That's
> the danger you face personally.
>
> But on top of that, it's my responsibility to ensure noth-
> ing happens to the thirty-seven Cubans who are here, to
> assure them proper living and working conditions, to
> make sure that there is harmony and stability within the
> brigade, that we hold high Cuba's name and prestige. It's
> not about a personal achievement—it's about the achieve-
> ment of continuing what Cuba and Cuban medicine rep-
> resent in the world.

Men like him don't abandon their posts

DR. GRACILIANO DÍAZ BARTOLA

He is a steady-going, obliging native of Santiago. His life's path has not been smooth, but it has been straight—he knew what direction he wanted to take. Dr. Graciliano Díaz is fifty-nine years old. His wife is an educator in day-care centers. He has four daughters and three grandchildren. All the daughters are university graduates: one has a degree in public health and epidemiology, one is a lawyer, another a sociologist. The youngest is in her third year of medical school.

He first became a medical-equipment technician in 1972, repairing oxygen machines and equipment for hospital operating rooms and therapy units. He was skilled in his field but dreamed of doing more. In 1978–84 he studied medicine and became a founder of Cuba's family doctor program in Granma province—after the initial doctors had started the pilot program at Havana's Lawton clinic. He completed that training in 1988.

Dr. Díaz's first internationalist mission, in 2002, was in Bolivia:

> That was before Evo Morales won the elections in 2005. It was during "Black October," the 2003 conflict in Bolivia where many people were killed.[1] We were working in the

---

1. In October 2003 the police and army in Bolivia, seeking to halt mass protests, killed dozens of workers and peasants. The popular revolt, however, forced the resignation of President Gonzalo Sánchez de Lozada.

area of La Higuera, Vallegrande province. It was a beauti-ful mission, because we were the first Cuban doctors to arrive in that country and in that region after the exhuma-tion of Che's remains. We were asked to do a number of things, including appear in a film and also a documentary along with Cuban actress Isabel Santos.

We were three doctors, and we covered the whole re-gion of Vallegrande—many of the places where Che had been—a very poor area that lacked electricity. We were there for twenty-five months. I met Chato Peredo, Inti's brother. Our encounters with him were very moving.[2]

Guinea, however, was his longest and most intense ex-perience as an internationalist doctor. Arriving July 25, 2011, he was one of fifteen Cuban general practitioners who were part of the Comprehensive Health Program there well before the Ebola outbreak. They worked in six regions: Labé, Kankan, Faranah, Mamou, Boké, and Cona-kry.

Dr. Díaz was following in the footsteps of the interna-tionalists of the 1960s and '70s, first in Vallegrande, Bolivia, and then in Boké, Guinea, near the border with Guinea-Bissau where the Cuban guerrilla doctors who fought un-der Amilcar Cabral had been posted. In mid-2012 he was transferred to Conakry as head of the brigade.

In 2014, when his return to Cuba was approaching, the Ebola epidemic broke out. He recalled a dramatic moment:

---

2. In 1966–67, Ernesto Che Guevara led a nucleus of revolutionaries from Bolivia, Cuba, and Peru, who fought to overthrow the military dictator-ship in Bolivia. Wounded and captured by US-trained Bolivian army forces, Guevara was murdered October 9, 1967, near the village of La Higuera. Guido "Inti" Peredo was one of the Bolivians in the guerrilla unit; his brother Osvaldo "Chato" Peredo was active in revolutionary politics in subsequent years.

One Monday morning I arrived at the internal medicine ward of the Donka Hospital, where I worked, and found there was only one nurse. When I asked about the doctors and interns—that is, the medical students—they told me there were none. The head of services had met on the first floor with some of the doctors because the head of the hospital's emergency department had died of Ebola. People were refusing to work.

So the head of services and I had to attend to the patients by ourselves. We made sure to protect ourselves well. We had received some prior training in Cuba as well as here.

We called people from Doctors Without Borders—who at that time were the ones specialized in such cases—to examine the patients in the hospital who were suspected of having Ebola.

Fear always exists; it never leaves you. We've had to be brave to confront a disease we weren't familiar with. And to do it in such a hostile environment from a public health standpoint, where the risks are not visible.

Dr. Graciliano's experience in the country, and the fact that on his own he had learned the Creole French spoken by Guineans, proved very useful to the newly arrived doctors and nurses of the Henry Reeve Contingent who, starting in October 2014, would confront the Ebola epidemic. Although he was already due to return home, he agreed to join the new brigade as its deputy head.

I met Dr. Graciliano in March 2015 at the Ebola Treatment Unit in Coyah, and on several occasions he served as our translator. Around that time he decided, once again, to postpone his return to Cuba. The president of Guinea had asked Cubans who were willing to do so to remain an additional month beyond the six months originally agreed to with WHO. It was during that final month that he suffered a heart attack. But he recovered and spent his post-hospital convalescence in the care of friends and colleagues, including ambassador Maité Rivero and third secretary Daffne Mirabal at their residence.

Men like him don't abandon their posts.

I've always liked to give my best

NURSE ROGELIO LABRADOR ALEMÁN

It was already midday when we arrived at La Hacienda Hotel in the town of Wonkifong, Guinea, near the Coyah Ebola Treatment Unit. Brigade members who were off shift invited us to lunch. It was then that Rogelio appeared, doubling as a cook, with his smile and his ever-present desire to serve. Later we learned that he was one of the most dedicated nurses.

This was not his first mission. He had been to Bolivia in 2002–2006 and had worked with the Henry Reeve Contingent during the fateful days of the Haiti earthquake. In that Caribbean country he had learned some French, and in the Coyah unit he got along well with the kitchen staff. As he would tell me later:

> In addition to other things, I took care of preparing food for people who got sick. It's very sad when you're separated from your family and no one provides personalized care for the patient. I had some kitchen experience; I prepared different kinds of meals: a soup or whatever the person wanted or needed. But I never stopped working at

"It is common knowledge that, through your internationalism programme, Cuban medical personnel are sent overseas. I call upon you to help us get out of this serious health crisis."

—Ernest Koroma, president of Sierra Leone
letter to Cuban president Raúl Castro, August 2014

Freetown, Sierra Leone, October 2014. Cuban medical volunteers unload supplies on arrival. "When we got there, the fatality rate for Ebola was 90 percent," said Dr. Manuel Seijas. "When we left it was 45%. Discipline and dedication helped turn that around."

"Different groups worked together. But the key to our capacity to fight the Ebola epidemic in Sierra Leone was the Cuban brigade."
—Andy Mason, Save the Children International

ESTUDIOS REVOLUCIÓN

ANTONIO PONS/BOHEMIA

Top: Havana, October 2014. Cuban president Raúl Castro, vice president José Ramón Machado Ventura, and minister of public health Roberto Morales see off medical brigade to Sierra Leone.

Bottom: Havana, 2014. Training session at Pedro Kourí Institute of Tropical Medicine before deployment. "Cuba is a small, poor country," says Ubieta. "But it offered doctors to treat Ebola before any other government."

Ebola epidemic:
Bred by imperialist plunder

	LIBERIA	SIERRA LEONE	GUINEA	CUBA 1950-59	2018
Infant deaths per 1,000 live births	56	117	65	37	4
Maternal deaths per 100,000 live births	990	860	980	138	44
HIV/AIDS per 100,000 inhabitants	521	965	1,031	—	161
Tuberculosis deaths per 100,000 people	495	1,304	274	14	0.2
Doctors per 100,000 inhabitants	1	2	(N/A)	10	848
Life expectancy (years)	62	46	58	57	78
Population with access to electricity	10%	14%	26%	56%	100%
Population with access to potable water	76%	63%	77%	64%	95%

SOURCES: WORLD HEALTH ORGANIZATION, WORLD BANK, CUBAN MINISTRY OF PUBLIC HEALTH

Above: Freetown, Sierra Leone, March 2015. Waiting for delivery of potable water.

"Everyone—doctors and nurses—had to perform IVs, wipe bottoms, and mop the floors. This norm was carried out to the letter." — Dr. Rotceh Ríos

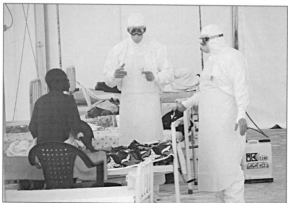

PHOTOS BY ENRIQUE UBIETA GÓMEZ

Top: Coyah treatment center, Guinea, January 2015. Cuban doctors and Guinean staff at shift change. "As they reported for duty, the Cubans always made jokes," says Ubieta. "It lifted their own spirits and those of patients and colleagues from other countries."

Bottom: Cuban physicians treating patients at Coyah. This center had the best survival rate, said Andy Mason, British director of the unit. "And the Cubans were vital in providing that painstaking care."

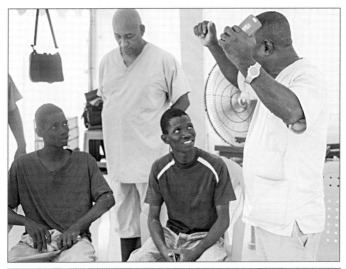

PHOTOS BY ENRIQUE UBIETA GÓMEZ

Top: Coyah center, Guinea, January 2015. Doctors with two patients who had won fight against Ebola. When Cuban volunteers first arrived at treatment centers, said Dr. Rotceh Ríos, "we had to change the idea that the patients couldn't be touched. When we began to treat them our way, more survived."

Bottom: Three patients at Coyah who recovered. Some former patients now immune to virus stayed on to work with the doctors. "They helped convince new patients to get treatment," said medic Osvaldo Miranda.

"When I told my wife I was going back to Sierra Leone, she told me it couldn't be any other way."
—Dr. Félix Báez

Dr. Félix Báez, part of the team in Sierra Leone, was the sole Cuban volunteer to contract Ebola during the mission.

Top: After initial treatment in Kerry Town, Báez was transferred to hospital in Switzerland. "Don't worry," he told fellow brigade members. "I'll come back so we can finish the mission."

Bottom: Báez, back at work in Sierra Leone, March 2015.

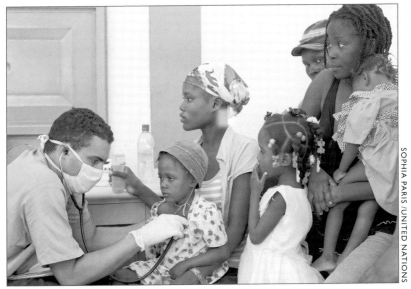

SOPHIA PARIS / UNITED NATIONS

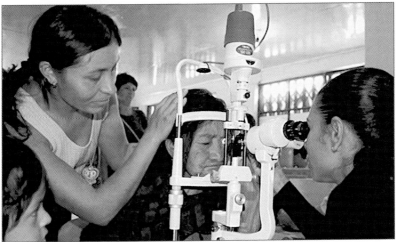

Top: Cuban doctor, one of hundreds serving in Haiti after 2010 earthquake, treats cholera patients in L'Estère, northern Haiti.

Bottom: Clinic in Bolivia, part of Cuba's "Operation Miracle." Over 12 years, volunteer Cuban surgeons there restored eyesight to more than 700,000 people.

"Some doctors at first wouldn't touch the patients. But when they saw Cubans do so, washing the patients and inserting IV lines, they said, 'Well, if you can do it, why can't we?'"

—Dr. Luis Escalona

CUBAN MEDICAL BRIGADE IN GUINEA/FACEBOOK PAGE

Above: Doctor with patients being released from Coyah center, Guinea. Altogether, 256 doctors, nurses, and health technicians were chosen to go to West Africa to fight Ebola epidemic. But some 12,000 had volunteered. "Solidarity is very much alive in the Cuban people," says Ubieta.

the center as a nurse. Also, they are Muslims, and there are dishes they don't eat such as pork, and those were the kinds of things I saw to.

Rogelio came from a peasant background. He lost his father when he was five. "My mother had three children from her first marriage and another six from the second." He still lives with her and a sister. As a child he dreamed of becoming an actor or singer and would practice in front of the television. But his mother steered him in other directions. He became a nurse, first with only a ninth-grade education, and then completed his pre-university studies at the Worker and Peasant School for adult education.

He enjoys nursing, saying, "I've always liked to give my best." He passed the entrance exams, attended the university and, after graduating, obtained a master's degree in urgent care.

One afternoon in September 2014, when the family had gathered to celebrate his mother's birthday, he took the opportunity to break the news: he had volunteered to travel to a West African country and contribute to the fight against Ebola. His brothers and sisters backed his decision. He proudly told me:

> One of them had fought in Angola. I told my mother, who was then turning ninety-three, that I would be going to Haiti to teach for a period of three to six months. She was very happy about that. To be honest, I had no idea what we would encounter. But I never felt afraid, maybe just a little stress.

After Doctors Without Borders refused to train Cuban brigade members in the red zone of the treatment center it ran, some of the Cuban doctors had to travel to a town 600 miles from the capital. Rogelio made the two-day journey. But they found no model institution there. The director who welcomed them was diagnosed with Ebola two or three days later. The conditions were terrible. The Cubans both learned and taught.

That center had been established despite opposition from the local community. Communication problems between the government and the population persisted. One morning riots broke out. Residents hijacked the vehicles of the doctors and nurses who were working at the treatment unit, and there were clashes with the police.

It was a rough experience, but Rogelio was undaunted. The deputy head of the brigade, Dr. Graciliano, who was in charge of that group, said he was surprised by Rogelio's calm and courageous behavior. As he had been in Bolivia and Haiti, Rogelio was named one of the most outstanding Cuban health workers in Guinea.

By the end of the mission my mom had already found out where I really was. When I returned, she went to meet me at the Provincial Health Administration for the welcome-home reception. She had been preparing for it for days and was very excited. Our return trip took longer than expected, and people told her, "Just wait for him at home."

"No," she replied. "Today my son the hero is arriving."

The women

Cuban authorities decided that only men would go. The risks to the health workers being sent were unknown. Statistical analyses, however, seemed to confirm the hypothesis, later rejected, that women were biologically more susceptible to contracting the virus. This decision upset hundreds of women doctors and nurses who were eager to participate.

Dr. Manuel Seijas, coordinator of the Cuban medical team at the Ebola Treatment Unit in Maforki–Port Loko, Sierra Leone, explained:

> We evaluated the work after two months, studying the patterns of the disease, and we observed that the virus showed no preference for age or sex. But the habits and customs of the country made women more vulnerable because of their role in daily life. Women had more interactions with others. They moved around the most among the population in search of food, doing household chores—and so

they were infected more frequently.

Women also suffered a higher death rate, not by much, but it was higher because women tended to be in worse physical condition. We saw that.

The same was true of children and the elderly, according to Dr. Seijas: "You hear about a life expectancy of forty-seven years. It was rare to see elderly people among the patients. There were some, but at both ends of the age range—people over sixty and children under five—death rates were much higher."

Among the reasons given for women not being part of the Ebola medical brigade, there was one that reflected the character of the mission: if there were a risk that some of those participating might not return home, it was preferable that they be men and not women, since the latter are the backbone of society. There were no discriminatory restrictions based on specific reasons of gender, sexual orientation, or faith. In the war against Ebola there was participation by all.

That's why I want to say a few words about two women who did not waver as they lived through the most intense periods of the epidemic. One was Cuba's ambassador to Guinea, Maité Rivero Torres, who remained at her post for the duration. Together with her husband, Daffne, she was there before the arrival of the Cuban medical volunteers and the international solidarity assistance, and stayed after the volunteers departed.

The other was Dr. Eneida Álvarez Horta, who served as head of the Comprehensive Health Program (CHP) brigade in Sierra Leone until the Henry Reeve Contingent arrived.

Dr. Geldys Rodríguez Palacio was in Guinea for a shorter stint, serving as head of the CHP brigade, but she too asked to stay and confront the perils of the epidemic. She replaced Dr. Graciliano Díaz, who completed his CHP assignment and enlisted as deputy head of the Henry Reeve Contingent that would fight Ebola.

Dr. Díaz, head of the CHP in Guinea when the epidemic began, told me, "I always kept ambassador Maité up-to-date about the epidemic. We really learned from her—as a person, as a Cuban, as a friend. She remained abreast of the Ebola situation from the beginning in March 2014."

Maité was well-respected among Guinean government officials, and that opened doors for us with ministers and intellectuals, as well as with the president of Guinea. They had seen her accompany Cuban doctors and nurses, and act as though she was just another Guinean. With her personal touch and modesty, she involved herself in all the activities of the brigade, which she regularly visited in Coyah. Despite her diplomatic rank, she served as our translator in official meetings. And she offered enthusiastic collaboration on this book from afar.

Maité was a Cuban in every sense of the word. The following anecdote tells you a lot about her. During a reception in honor of the Orquesta Aragón during the Cuban band's visit to Guinea, which of course ended with a brief concert, the president, a very circumspect person, invited her to dance. Maité is an accomplished salsa dancer, and the images of that dance were broadcast over and over on national television.

President Alpha Condé told us, laughing, "The wife of Mali's president called me and said, 'How is it that Orquesta Aragón comes to Guinea and you dance with the Cuban ambassador, but you don't invite me to come and dance too?' Here in Guinea people called me asking, 'Why are you dancing with the Cuban ambassador and not with us?'

"'She's my dance partner. We Guineans have grown up with Cuban music,' I said."

One day she received an unusual invitation to attend a meeting of ambassadors to Guinea from other African countries. The president explained to her, "Cuba is Africa." She was liked and respected by everyone.

On completing her diplomatic mission in November 2015, Maité Rivero received the National Order of Merit of the Republic of Guinea, with the rank of commander, for her contributions to the friendship between the Cuban and Guinean peoples. In her words of acknowledgment she said, "We feel this medal of honor also belongs to all the Cuban volunteers who have carried out missions in this country, especially those in the health sector and in particular the thirty-eight doctors and nurses who, under the auspices of the World Health Organization, came to fight the Ebola epidemic, even at the risk of their own lives."

There is also much to be said about Dr. Eneida Álvarez Horta and her fellow volunteers in Sierra Leone. In May 2014, when the health brigade returned from vacations at home in Cuba, the press was talking about an Ebola epidemic only in the neighboring countries of Guinea and Liberia. Sierra Leone officials apparently were concealing the presence of the disease. She told me:

> In late May the atmosphere was becoming tense in the office of Dr. Maya Conteh, the health ministry coordinator for the project, but they didn't talk about it in front of me. I was worried. I knew something was happening, and it was related to Ebola. Every day I would work through the problems of the brigade with him. As soon as some were resolved, others would appear. We would meet before I did my patient visits or after I finished them.
>
> My driver already knew people were dying in Kailahun

district, 75 miles from Kenema district, where I had three health workers posted. And Kailahun was 105 miles from Liberia. Kenema and Liberia were connected by a 175-mile stretch of highway. For me all this information was very important because in Liberia the epidemic was out of control and people were fleeing toward Kailahun. As I explained before, the sick were dying and no one knew the cause, because many didn't go to the hospital out of fear. They would flee into the forest and die there. Besides, the symptoms were similar to those of malaria, an endemic disease in Sierra Leone and other African countries.

In early June I met with the coordinator, and the first point of discussion was Ebola. "Since we arrived," I told him, "I've heard talk that there are cases of Ebola in Kailahun district. I want you to tell me the truth. And if you're keeping information from me out of fear that Cuba will pull out the brigade, don't worry. I'm convinced we're not going to leave. Cuba's position has always been to send reinforcements—not to withdraw our personnel." I told him the story of cholera in Haiti and the earthquake there.

Then he told me it was true. There were many dead in that district, but they weren't certain because they didn't have the means to do the tests there. The samples were being sent to Kenema district, where the only laboratory for Lassa fever [a hemorrhagic fever] in the country was located, and where the best virologist was working. Some cases were turning out positive. I had three volunteers working in that hospital, two women and a man.

From that moment, Ebola began its conquest across the territory. And Dr. Eneida Álvarez, going around everywhere, put the brakes on everyone who felt inclined to abandon the mission. She visited the health workers she was responsible for, reported to Cuba, and received instructions. She distributed the special suits and made sure everyone knew the safety guidelines that had been learned in Havana.

They faced difficult situations, such as that of the anesthesiologist working in the operating room of the maternity hospital. A sick woman was admitted in very poor condition, bleeding. The health worker had to administer metoclopramide [an antinausea drug] intravenously and take her blood pressure. The woman died the next day, and the test confirmed she had Ebola. The anesthesiologist was immediately quarantined, and the situation was reported to Havana. But she had used the suit correctly and followed the proper procedure.

The reports from the hospitals were ominous:

> Patients were dying in the general medicine wards, and only several days later was it noted that they had Ebola and not malaria. But the Cuban volunteers were very disciplined in complying with the safety measures. They did not evacuate—who then would have taken care of the children and pregnant women?

In the capital, the response to the virus wasn't organized any better, Dr. Eneida explained:

> When the epidemic reached the capital, a Sierra Leonean doctor fell ill and died in Connaught Hospital, just from holding a woman who had fainted because she had Ebola. All the sick people were in the room waiting to be seen, and confusion reigned. There was no triage. It was through that room that we entered, the four of us—a maxillofacial surgeon, a medical-equipment technician, a dermatologist, and an ear, nose, and throat specialist.
> After the doctor died, the hospital went on strike and

shut down almost all services. Local staff members refused to work because of the risk of contagion, but we continued to provide medical care. We no longer came in through that room, but instead through another entrance. Patients were asking to be discharged; barely any were left. Several triage nurses working in the emergency department died. The situation was becoming more difficult every day. Patients were coming to see the ear, nose, and throat doctor who were bleeding and whose symptoms had nothing to do with that specialty. The maxillofacial surgeon was getting patients who had a fever and were in very poor condition. And patients were coming to see me, the dermatologist, with gynecological problems and other symptoms.

We knew the nurses were not separating them by condition, and there were only two doctors, from an NGO, working in the emergency department. Patients were collapsing in the hallway where the ear, nose, and throat doctor and I had our examination rooms, and when they were taken to the emergency room they died of Ebola.

The male members of the brigade felt compelled to act by the example being set by the women. Dr. Jacinto del Llano Rodríguez, who had previously served in Gambia and Venezuela, acknowledged the courage of his female co-workers:

At some point we felt fear. It's a very difficult disease, it was unknown, there was no specific treatment. But we're Cubans and we've experienced other crises. The women were a pillar of strength. They didn't want to leave—they wanted to complete the mission that was scheduled to end in April 2015. All the men and women expressed our readiness to transfer to the Ebola brigade if needed.

This opinion was shared and expanded on by the brigade's medical-equipment technician, Pedro Luis Ferreira Betancourt, sixty, who had previously carried out missions in Mozambique and Honduras:

> Our brigade leader was always very concerned that everyone comply with the safety measures. I went on two tours of the provinces with her to reinforce that, but the women in particular demonstrated how outstanding they were. I was in Kenema in August, when the first hotspot emerged. There were two compañeras there, and their response was to stay and ask that they not be transferred somewhere else. There is always someone who is more afraid than the others, but neither one left her post. Neither woman wavered. The news that they would have to leave the mission was quite unexpected.

That's why the decision that the women return to Cuba— taken in October, when the epidemic was beginning to decline—was so hard. Dr. Eneida, forceful as always, sent a letter addressed to the Cuban public health ministry, which appears below because it captures the feelings of these exemplary Cuban women:

> Dear compañeros:
>   At a special meeting of the board of directors, to which I belong as head of the permanent Cuban Medical Brigade in Sierra Leone, convened by the leadership of the Cuban mission, I received with astonishment and dismay the sad news of the immediate withdrawal of the women who are part of our brigade. The majority of them have been providing services here for more than two years and have won the admiration and respect of our compañeros, of the people of Sierra Leone, and of the public

health and political authorities.

From the beginning of the Ebola epidemic, women have remained firm and faithful to the ideas of Fidel, Raúl, our parents, and the revolution, convinced that we would never abandon the people of this country in the midst of the difficult times they are going through.

During the months of July, August, and September, when circumstances regarding the epidemic became more difficult and we were practically alone in this country, we remained in daily communication with Cuban health workers, and the women always responded bravely and positively. Not one abandoned her post, and some took on the work of foreign and local medical personnel who left due to fear of the epidemic.

We visited Kenema, the second hotspot in those days, to assess whether our fellow Cubans in that district should remain. The response by Dr. Vanesa, Dr. Larramendi, and Teresa, the nurse, was very inspiring—they would continue maximizing safety measures in order to stay there, where they were so needed.

I never received a single complaint from any of our compañeras, not even at the moments of greatest danger, when even some of our men hesitated to remain at their jobs for fear of contagion.

We will comply in disciplined fashion with the decisions of our superiors. But I believe at this very moment—with the epidemic noticeably receding, as official reports indicate, and with adequate safety measures in place and the encouraging presence of the medical brigade from the Henry Reeve Contingent and a permanent representative of the Cuban foreign ministry—we deserve a vote of confidence to be able to fully meet our commitment just like the men.

I have not yet been authorized to communicate this

latest decision to the rest of the compañeras, but I am convinced they will all share my views.

The most fitting recognition of our efforts and devotion would be for all of us, men and women, to return together to our homeland in April, with the immense pride of a duty fulfilled, as worthy heirs of Mariana Grajales, Celia Sánchez, Vilma Espín, and so many other heroines who throughout the glorious years of the revolution have given the best of themselves—to hold high the name of Cuban women.*

With revolutionary greetings,
Dr. Eneida Álvarez Horta
Coordinator, Permanent Cuban
Medical Brigade in Sierra Leone

Despite this heartfelt letter, all the women who were in Guinea and Sierra Leone were called back to Cuba. After arriving they were awarded the August 23 Order by the Federation of Cuban Women. All women and men working in the Ebola-affected countries as part of the Comprehensive Health Program were also awarded the Labor Achievement Medal. The majority of women then left to carry out new internationalist missions in other countries. As I write these lines, Dr. Eneida is in Mozambique.

It's also essential that I devote a few words to the wives and mothers of the Cuban brigade members. Some were pregnant when their husbands left, and their children were born while their husbands were being exposed to

---

* Mariana Grajales was a heroine of Cuba's nineteenth-century independence wars. Celia Sánchez and Vilma Espín were leaders of the July 26 Movement and Rebel Army combatants in the revolutionary war against the Batista dictatorship. Both held central leadership responsibilities after the 1959 revolutionary victory.

Ebola in West Africa. Others had young children, one or two months old. They were all affected by the selection of their companions or sons for a mission that was regarded as suicidal. Yet the majority supported them. All grieved the death from malaria of two of the volunteers, Jorge Juan Guerra and Coqui—Reinaldo Villafranca—and were concerned about Félix Báez's illness, as if they had been their own companions or sons.

The wives and mothers hold a whole range of different jobs—a result of the fact that in Cuba two thirds of university graduates are women. They had to shoulder all the social and family responsibilities they normally shared with their companions.

As president Raúl Castro underscored at the "Global Leaders' Meeting on Gender Equality and Women's Empowerment: A Commitment to Action," held in New York on September 27, 2015:

> Today life expectancy at birth for Cuban women is 80.4 years of age. The direct maternal mortality rate [deaths from complications in childbirth] is only 21.4 per 100,000 live births, one of the lowest in the world.
>
> Cuban women are 48 percent of the total number working in the state civil sector, and hold 46 percent of high leadership positions. They account for 78.5 percent of health-care personnel, 48 percent of scientific researchers, and 66.8 percent of the workforce with the highest technical and professional qualifications. Cuban women on average complete the 10th grade of schooling and they account for 65.2 percent of graduates in higher education.

Those who fell

Anti-Cuban propaganda predicted that our doctors and nurses would become infected and die of Ebola. These were macabre assumptions but based on a very real fact—other foreign brigades, which were smaller and stayed only four to six weeks, had all seen some of their members become infected and die. Of the 256 Cuban brigade members who were exposed to the virus for six months, only one contracted the disease and he survived. Not a single case of Ebola was detected in Cuba, thanks to the safety measures implemented.

Fate struck the Cuban brigade from an unforeseen direction, however. Two of its members died suddenly—one in Guinea, the other in Sierra Leone—from the deadliest and most intractable disease on the continent: malaria. In both cases they suffered cerebral complications.

The most recent statistics available, according to the World Health Organization, show that in 2012 some 612,000 people died of malaria worldwide, 90 percent of them in

Africa. The disease, which can be cured and is preventable, continues to claim lives there. The Cubans who fell in this battle were Jorge Juan Guerra, who was responsible for finances (each brigade included someone with that assignment), and Reinaldo Villafranca Lantigua, a nurse known by the nickname "Coqui."

JORGE JUAN GUERRA RODRÍGUEZ

Castro Baras, head of the brigade in Guinea, recalled the first time he met Jorge Juan Guerra:

> One day I was on my way to the Pedro Kourí Institute, where we were getting excellent training, limited only by the lack of patients. Jorge Juan Guerra approached me. He worked as a statistician at the Provincial Health Administration in Sancti Spíritus.
>
> He stepped up to me and said, "Colonel, I'm going be handling finances on the Guinea brigade. You're going to be my boss."
>
> "OK . . . and who are you?" I asked.
>
> "I'm Jorge Guerra from Sancti Spíritus."
>
> At first I thought he was joking, but that's how I found out I was going to head up the mission. I was informed later that day, but it seems the news had leaked out beforehand.
>
> I half-jokingly replied, "Well, no one's told me, but if I'm going to be your boss, welcome aboard." That's how we met and began to share those first few days.

Guerra was a sprightly man who always carried a small backpack on his shoulders. He was nearly sixty, although he didn't look it. On October 1, at 9:05 p.m., Guerra left for

Conakry—what was to be his life's final destination—via Sierra Leone. He was part of the leadership team that, together with Castro Baras and Carlitos, who was in charge of logistics, would get things set up for the arrival of the rest of the brigade. Dr. Graciliano Díaz, deputy head of the team in Guinea, was expecting them. They were on the flight taking all the volunteers assigned to Sierra Leone plus the Liberia leadership team. The latter was made up of Doctors Dupuy and Raventós; Andrés Marrero, in charge of finances; and Rolando Vergara, responsible for logistics.

Traveling on that plane as part of the Sierra Leone brigade was nurse Reinaldo Villafranca Lantigua—Coqui—the other Cuban who months later would die of malaria. These two men who would both soon meet their death—did they happen to talk to each other during that long flight? Perhaps a simple "pardon me" while walking down the narrow aisle? They barely knew each other, although they had trained together at the Kourí Institute. They were seen off at the foot of the plane by Army General Raúl Castro.

They arrived in Freetown October 2 and in Conakry October 6, after a stopover in Morocco. The four members of the "advance party" and Ambassador Maité prepared everything for the arrival of the rest of the brigade on October 22.

Castro Baras continued his account:

On October 23 Jorge Juan Guerra turned sixty, and we celebrated with a cake, but no alcoholic beverages. We sang happy birthday for him. He was delighted—we have pictures capturing the moment. By the next day he said he wasn't feeling well. Two days earlier he had had diarrhea, but he ate a lot, especially sweets. We placed him under medical care, but his health deteriorated rapidly. We did a malaria test and it came back positive. We immediately started treatment for him at the hotel. We asked WHO authorities to transfer him to a hospital, and they arranged for him to be admitted to a private clinic. That night he took a sharp turn for the worse. On October 26, at 6:00 p.m., he died.

We later learned Jorge had previously contracted cerebral malaria during a mission in Mali. His death really hit us hard, the other brigade members more than us, since they had just arrived, and their "welcome" was the death of a co-worker. We had put him on a round-the-clock watch that many doctors and nurses were part of, fighting hard to save his life.

I was able to speak with the first and the last doctors to care for Jorge. José Eduardo Díaz Gómez, a specialist in comprehensive general medicine and intensive care from Havana, recalled, "I spent the first night at the hospital, and we worked hard on him, with everything intensive care involves, all the medications, making sure he lacked nothing. But he rapidly suffered multiple organ failure." Dr. Jorge Luis Lucas Delgado, an intensive-care and internal medicine specialist from Santiago, was the last doctor at his bedside:

> The night of October 25 he fell into a coma, and the next day it was my turn to tend to him in intensive care. WHO had arranged with a foreign hospital to transfer him in order to perform kidney dialysis and try to save his life, but he couldn't hang on. I spent the final hours with him, along with another compañero. It was a huge blow. Remember, in Cuba everyone was telling us we were crazy because we were going to defy death and on arriving, a colleague dies. There we realized how serious this was, because we were facing deadly diseases.

Guinea is a country with an Islamic culture and people are buried directly in the ground. So a coffin had to be ordered, and a grave opened and sealed in the cemetery, to ensure that his remains would be preserved and could later be sent back home.

Cuban ambassador Maité Rivero Torres recalled those painful days:

> Early that October 26, we received a call from Castro Baras informing us that our co-worker's condition had seriously deteriorated. We immediately called the Guinean ministers of cooperation and health. They responded even though it was a Sunday—a very important day for Guinean families—and went with us to the clinic. They stayed with us all day, until our colleague died around six p.m. Then they went with us to the morgue, helped with the funeral arrangements and everything that followed, and finally, attended our tribute to him November 1.
>
> I think this showed the Guinean government's high regard for the Cuban volunteer effort and for what it meant that these men made such a sacrifice, coming from their country, and in this case, unfortunately, losing their lives.

The first lady, accompanied by ministers' wives, visited the Cuban ambassador at her residence to express their condolences. A delegation from Guinea's National Assembly, headed by its first vice president, also visited the ambassador.

His mind full of memories, Dr. José Eduardo Díaz recalled both the best and worst moments of those months:

> I can tell you it was the worst experience we went through. The most beautiful experience was to see a two-year-old boy, who had just pulled through six or seven days in very

serious condition, watch him play with a balloon we had made for him from a glove, laugh, and ask us for oranges and things. That was really beautiful. He had lost his mom, and his dad was waiting for him outside.

Castro Baras explained it this way: "We were able to overcome the initial impact and turn it into energy that reinforced our work. Whenever we are able to, we go to the cemetery to pay tribute to our brother who fell in the line of duty."

I too visited his grave and observed a moment of silence.

REINALDO VILLAFRANCA LANTIGUA, 'COQUI'

Coqui wasn't born lucky. He overcame obstacles through sheer willpower. He was drifting through life when the revolution extended a helping hand. I'm not overstating the importance of that hand; many don't grasp it when they have the chance—without the will to save yourself, nobody is saved—but Coqui held onto it like a castaway. He began to study nursing thanks to Fidel's project to rescue youth who were neither working nor studying.* Some of his teachers were younger than he was. He began to discover what he had inside him: he had a deep-going vocation for

---

* At Fidel Castro's initiative, Cuba's revolutionary leadership launched a political offensive in 2000, known as the Battle of Ideas, that sought to broaden educational and cultural opportunities. It also aimed to combat social inequalities that had widened as Cuba became more directly exposed to the capitalist world market after the collapse of its preferential trade relations with Soviet-bloc countries a decade earlier. This included efforts to involve youth who had dropped out of school and were not working. The government provided them with stipends to study as well as jobs.

nursing, an inner desire to be useful.

José Raúl Milán, one of his professors and a fellow nurse in the battle against Ebola, recalled what he was like back then: "He was a regular guy, very jovial, who loved to tell stories—sometimes I had to remind him that we were in class."

It wasn't easy. At one point Coqui became discouraged and was close to giving up. "Twice I went to see him at home," José Raúl said, "because he wanted to drop out of the course. On those visits I saw the hardships, the deprivations he faced. I knew he had a future as a nurse. He was very humble but very intelligent, exemplary in his selflessness and willpower."

Reinaldo obtained his nursing license. With that impetus, he went on to get a postgraduate degree. Above all, he won the affection of his co-workers and patients at the clinic in his hometown of Los Palacios, in Pinar del Río province. Coqui had much to contribute to others and to fulfill in his own life.

When he heard about the Ebola outbreak, he was one of the first to volunteer. Nurse Víctor Lázaro Guerra Viera saw him arrive one overcast, rainy day, completely drenched, at the Provincial Medical Cooperation Unit. He had come to sign up for the group that hoped to be part of the brigade of anti-Ebola combatants:

> That day there was a tremendous downpour. He came from the town of Los Palacios to bring his file. He told me he had come straight from working night shift, was tired, and had to return by bus or hitching a ride—he lived far away. As he was leaving under that downpour, we began to review his file and saw that some things were missing. They said, "Go tell him." I caught up with him and had him come back. That's how I met Coqui.

Those who knew him from earlier years would never have imagined that he would be the only passenger boarding the bus in Los Palacios. He left his mother a sow that had just given birth so she could make a little money in his absence. He stood out during the training not only for his skills as a nurse but for his knowledge of English, which he had taught himself in another life. He lent his former teachers his collection of "English Without Borders" CDs, which no one knows how he acquired.

But he was afraid he wouldn't be selected, since there were three hundred candidates, many of them with more years of experience and previous missions under their belts. He suffered from high blood pressure, so his friends helped him calm his nerves during the medical checkup. He was finally chosen, despite his sketchy résumé. Nurse Juan Carlos Curbelo Fajardo witnessed that moment:

> He was one of the first to try out the suit, the Personal Protective Equipment, and did it well. He showed competency. When we were chosen among the 103 nurses who would travel to Sierra Leone, Coqui felt proud, and cried as he left the theater. He told me he hadn't thought he would make the cut.

Coqui had never traveled by plane and was scared. Juan Carlos, his former professor and now a co-worker, sat next to him and let him grab his hand whenever there was a bump, just as Coqui had done when he grabbed the opportunity to study at the university. A new stage in his life was beginning. He felt part of a group that accepted him as he was, not trying to change him. He confronted death without losing his smile, as heroes do.

"Coqui had a tremendous, lively spirit," Víctor Lázaro recalled. "You wondered where he got so much energy and strength because, when some got tired, he always remained alert, attentive, kidding around. Those who worked in Kerry Town told us he was a workhorse, fearless." Villafranca wanted to excel and reshape his future. Yes, that meant freeing himself from the "prison" of material limitations and improving conditions for him and his mother. But it also meant developing a new social outlook, remaking himself as a person. He more than achieved that. The illness—the specter both feared and accepted by brigade members—took him by surprise. Juan Carlos recalled:

> Right after it was decided he would be transferred to Kerry Town, we all began to talk among ourselves, especially with Frank Hernández Leyva, who was the person closest to him. They had been friends while he was living in the Compañero Hotel, even though they were in different rooms. Frank told me Coqui had just been taken away with all those symptoms.
>
> By Sunday morning he reported that Coqui's condition was critical and deteriorating. They were waiting to do a second Ebola test—the first one had been negative, and this one would determine whether he would be transferred to a British navy ship anchored out at sea to receive a more specialized treatment for his illness. The news came as a shock to all of us. We knew what had happened with the compañero in Guinea.

The impact of Coqui's brief stay at the Ebola Treatment Unit was enormous. His sudden death shook all the Cubans and their co-workers of other nationalities. As his friend Frank described him, "He was a cheerful person, very committed to his work. . . . He endeared himself to everyone, and was attuned to the mood of everyone around him." The doctors and especially the nurses from the African Union, whom he had generously taught what he knew, were in tears as they bid him farewell, lining both sides of the road as the coffin passed by. Juan Carlos reported:

> Dr. Félix returned January 15, and Coqui died almost at the same time. At the time we had been getting an infusion of moral incentives, patriotism, a sense of belonging—and then Coqui's death hit us. But that didn't lessen our sense of responsibility, nor did it affect our decision to remain there.

One journalist attempted to use Coqui's background to discredit the heroic nature of his death. To tell the truth, only a cynic with an utter lack of faith in human beings could ignore the new, genuine Villafranca that Coqui, with so much determination, had forged without ceasing to be the person he had always been. The journalist painted a false Villafranca based on his marginal background. To interpret his actions based on that starting point is to ignore the hard road he traveled. To rob him of the title of hero, based on a superficial view of his motivations, is to strip his death, and his life, of its meaning. That cynical journalist was not describing Coqui, only himself.

Ebola: Cultural and communication factors

The school year in Liberia, suspended for ten months, was now resuming. The most varied school uniforms filled the streets of the capital again. We visited a public high school there. The kids, alerted by the teachers as to why we were there, watched us with amusement and let us photograph them, but with a wide range of expressions: curiosity, defiance, flirtatiousness, distrust, playfulness.

We had interrupted classes and asked if we could interview one of the students. Without hesitation, the teacher chose a 15-year-old with piercing eyes. Very serious, she answered our questions with maturity and had plenty to say. The images my TV crew captured show some mischievous classmates making fun of us behind her. But what we are drawn to is the student: composed in front of the camera, her intelligent eyes seem to open and close to deeper thoughts. The young woman, Abigail, does not accept the premise that the animals cited by the press are the source of the disease.

The translator, one of the brigade doctors, asks again, confused—she is speaking very quickly, in Creole English. But she insists: "They said that killing and eating those animals brought this disease, but you know, I'm not really convinced. I don't think mongooses, monkeys, and bats could have caused it."

For several weeks I thought her answer was due to the influence of deep-rooted cultural traditions. My view was reinforced by Saran Daraba Kaba, general secretary of the Mano River Union, who said the governments of the three countries affected by Ebola had made many mistakes in how they informed people about the virus and about ways to deal with it:

> The people living in the area where the epidemic emerged— a forested region—don't have access to much animal protein. They don't raise livestock because conditions preclude it. So they eat meat from wild animals. And because of the Ebola epidemic we tell them, "No, that meat can't be eaten."
>
> But what alternatives do they have? We haven't given them any. We simply tell them, "You have to stop eating that kind of meat." But they've eaten it for centuries—their parents ate it, their grandparents ate it. So, if you ask them not to eat that meat, you're suspect. "Why are you asking me not to eat what all my ancestors have eaten? They never got sick, why would I get sick now?" And if that message comes from a white-skinned foreigner, something is wrong; they cannot be trusted.

The history of human interactions with bats is surprising. A recent science documentary reported that almost all cultures have some connection to that winged rodent. According to a December 10, 2015, report by the EFE news agency, "Dr. Carles Flaquer, a biologist, and Xavier Puig, an environmentalist, saw bat hospitals in Australia, vampire bats in Mexico, kitchens that cook the flying mammal in Bali, Indonesia, conservation projects in France and Catalonia, excursion sites to observe them in Texas, and lesser known tourist routes for the general public in Zambia."

But the problem pointed to by Kaba, as she herself suggests, goes beyond a simply cultural approach or communications policy. That's why anthropologist Adame Cerón doesn't attribute this behavior to traditional cultural practices. According to him, the accelerating deforestation of the African savanna—a process that several multinational agricultural corporations are involved in—wipes out small-scale farming and forces villagers to seek other sources of food:

> This leads vulnerable communities in the surrounding areas to come into contact with potentially dangerous animals as they try to feed themselves, venturing further and further into the tropical forests in search of them. The lack of protein sources increasingly pushes them to consume meat from the savanna—monkeys, small rodents, bats, etc.—which exposes them to new pathogens. (Adame Cerón, p. 170)

I find it interesting to look at errors the three governments made in their initial communications strategy—something they are aware of—which was often the result of external pressure. The reaction in international media was one of panic, especially after hospitals in the First World reported cases of foreign health workers and travelers who, after passing through health screenings at borders, were showing symptoms of infection. The images were terrifying.

Ebola was reported as incurable. As a result, many Africans who became sick argued that it was preferable to die at home, accompanied by their families. Sometimes patients who had been treated in specialized centers were rejected by their communities and expelled—God may have saved them, but they had been touched by the devil. They were forced to go deep into the forest and live in isolation.

The explanations and warnings in the press and on city billboards were all in English or French. A significant percentage of the population, however, did not read or write, and a substantial number spoke only their own dialect. The written word also faced another major cultural obstacle. As González López and Pulido Escandell wrote:

> The persistence of a vigorous oral culture and the rejection of written communication in some rural areas of Africa, a defensive reaction against a means the colonizers had used as a weapon against them: from the title deeds through which they were deprived of the land, to the notebooks used by the tax collectors. (*Cuadernos África–América Latina*, no. 27–28, 1997)

In addition, once the symptoms appeared, a person suffering from Ebola could only be saved if he or she went immediately to a specialized medical center, but that was not the usual practice. Saran Daraba Kaba noted:

> The first recourse by people in that area is self-medication, and if that doesn't work, they consult the traditional healer. Only when the illness persists do they go to the hospital, if there is one.
>
> That is why the people must be the primary focus of the communications strategy. They must understand what Ebola is, not with terrifying images such as those broad-

cast on television, with those strange men in special suits, but with simple words.

You have to explain to people that Ebola is a deadly disease, but that we catch it only if we are in contact with the sick person at the contagious stage of the disease.

You have to tell the peasants, the traders, the taxi drivers, the women. They are all very important observers in the community. They are up-to-date on everything that happens in the community, and when they go to market they interact and talk with neighbors. But above all you have to tell the religious leaders, the traditional leaders, the healers.

This was precisely one of the most glaring flaws: at first the healers and religious leaders were not drawn into the campaign against Ebola. In Guinea and Sierra Leone, both majority-Muslim countries, the imam is a community leader who cannot be ignored.

Imagine this scene: a child in the household falls sick. His symptoms at first resemble those of a simple cold, but men dressed like "astronauts" say it could be Ebola and they take the child to a mysterious center to which his family members have no access. One morning, someone informs them that he died and was buried in an unspecified place to prevent further spread of the illness. Neither the healer, whose pride is wounded, nor the imam, have been informed. The result can be explosive.

At first, as a result of such misunderstandings, people opposed building and operating the Ebola Treatment Units. A terrifying rumor spread, which despite the facts had a perverse historical logic: the disease didn't really exist and people were being killed in those centers to remove and sell their organs.

When people are uninformed, rumors make them particularly susceptible—conveniently so for the exploiters. Similar to a person suffering from jealousy, they sometimes project distrust toward everything and prevent the actual "adulterous relationship" from being identified. Some people who were sick fled into the bush or hid their symptoms. If there was speculation in the Western media about the supposedly intentional origin of the spread of the Ebola virus, how could it not be expected that the natural mistrust of people who have been historically manipulated and oppressed, combined with misinformation, would produce a hostile response?

In the Guinean town of Wonkifong, a woman arrived home one morning and couldn't find her husband. Someone told her he had been taken to the Ebola Treatment Unit in Coyah, a few miles away, and she went crazy. She roused the neighbors, giving them a macabre account of what had happened.

Everyone was in the streets, enraged, when a small bus passed through, the one that every morning took the Cuban doctors and nurses to the treatment unit. It could have been African Union health workers, or even Guinean doctors and nurses, but it happened to be Cubans. People didn't even know who was inside. Residents blocked the road and attacked the bus with stones, sticks, and machetes. They broke the windshield and other windows; some shards of glass slightly injured two Cuban volunteers, doctors Yoel Fleites and Eliéser Escalona.

The driver frantically turned the bus around and returned to the hotel where they were staying. The police arrived, restored order, and by the end of the day everything became clear: the husband had been drunk and spent the night in the street.

Dr. Carlos Castro Baras, head of the medical brigade in Guinea, told us how the Cuban part of the story ended:

It was certainly shocking and traumatic for the brigade. We took the first group back to the hotel, they were seen to, and the authorities came over. From then on, they provided us with security.

The very same day, at 8:00 p.m., the second group arrived in the treatment unit with 100 percent of its members—that's the kind of people the Cubans were. They worked into the early morning hours as if nothing had happened. They knew that the only ones who were not to blame for what had happened were the patients, and they could not be neglected. That's what we came here for—to work.

Sometimes relatives tried to find the burial site to recover the body, because according to tradition the body must be washed and properly shrouded. The body of the deceased, destroyed by the virus, is the greatest source of contamination—it's drained of fluids, which carry the contaminating virus. Mourners anoint themselves with the water used to wash the body, because that way they will acquire the best of the deceased person. At each traditional burial of someone who died of Ebola, ten to sixteen relatives and friends would become infected.

Dr. Manuel Seijas, who coordinated the group of Cubans at Maforki–Port Loko in Sierra Leone, reported that on one occasion twenty-four people infected at a burial arrived at once at the center; twelve of them died. On another occasion, seventeen arrived and eight died. But there are no solutions that can be imposed by force. The problem is of a cultural nature, and the only effective solution must be along those lines.

Senegalese anthropologist Cheikh Ibrahima Niang, of Dakar's Cheikh Anta Diop University, was commissioned by WHO to conduct a study of the behavior and customs of communities affected by Ebola. He wrote the following about the burials in a May 2015 article posted to the WHO website:

> In these communities, a dead person has rights and communities have certain obligations toward the deceased. If these rights are not respected, people lose credibility and respect in their communities. This is very important. . . .
>
> Washing the dead bodies of loved ones is not only an act of caring, but a purification rite and metaphor. The body has to be clean so the person is pure when he or she goes to heaven. The strings around the shroud are another metaphor: when the deceased unties these strings, his or her soul is freed and ascends. And the lightness of this ascending soul is yet another metaphor; the deceased has released any anger and anxiety that was weighing him or her down.
>
> There were also some conceptual clashes around diagnostics and treatment. For example, when you give blood, when you give lab samples, these things express the person as a whole. In addition, they do not belong only to the individual, but also to the community. The body is collective and the community has some responsibility to the collective. Community and group leaders in Kailahun insisted on confirming with their own eyes that there were no missing body parts before a dead person was buried.*

The Cuban doctors and nurses came in order to halt the devastating death toll that epidemics bring on, but they couldn't go beyond the limits of the hospital, of the patient. Dr. Carlos Castro Baras knew they were the last link in the chain and stated categorically:

---

* See list of references at the end of this book.

We can fight for the lives of patients, but an epidemic is defeated on the ground by actions taken with the people, cutting off contacts with those infected, tracking the chain of transmission, raising awareness among them. I would say the work we do registers the failure of the system: when a patient arrives at a treatment center, it's because the chain of transmission could not be stopped.

"In order to break the chain of transmission, it's not enough to treat the patient. You need to target two other factors: the mode of transmission and those who are susceptible to infection," noted Dr. Osvaldo Miranda Gómez, an epidemiologist who was studying for a second degree as a biostatistician. Having obtained his doctorate two years earlier at age thirty-six, he was now carrying out his second mission in Guinea as part of the Henry Reeve Contingent. In 2005 he had gone to Pakistan on a mission to halt an epidemic in the wake of the earthquake that devastated large areas of that country.

Dr. Miranda also knew, however, that the kind of treatment a patient receives in a hospital has an impact on the community:

The patients all arrive scared. It's understandable. They know that it's a deadly disease, that they may die. They think we're going to attack them, and many come to the hospital telling themselves that they will refuse to take any medicine or water we give them.

Now, the antidote to this fear is the patients themselves—those who've been in the hospital longer. One will tell the other, "Listen, these people can help you." And many of the patients whose lives we saved stay to work with us. It's a very rewarding experience, because they're the ones who help convince new patients.

One afternoon there were about five or six patients gathered together. They were happy because they knew they would be discharged the following day. We had a cell phone playing music, and we started to joke around and sing, and they started dancing. It was nice, because some of them had come to the treatment center in serious condition. Next to them there were doctors wearing their suits. But we were on the other side of the fence, which allowed the patient to see our faces and recognize us—with the special suit on we all looked alike.

Guinean authorities acknowledged the importance of the communication process and the mistaken way it had been carried out. By February and March 2015 they had begun to correct it. President Alpha Condé told us:

The other challenge we've had is that the health workers we sent to carry out the work of raising awareness hired staff from the NGOs. But if you're a foreigner and you go to an area where you're not known, you'll have a hard time convincing people. We have to use people from those areas—such as healers, elders, imams—because they can easily communicate with the population. Fortunately we've now corrected that error.

The result was an absurd, damaging struggle between the people and the authorities in which the former managed to get around all the health measures established by the latter. "Angry, frustrated, frightened by this disease that was killing them, and by recommendations that clashed with their belief systems, they felt misunderstood and abandoned by the whole world," anthropologist Cheikh Ibrahima Niang noted.

It was said that one day a taxi arrived at a checkpoint

with three passengers in the back seat. All three sat very upright and were well dressed; the passenger in the middle was a corpse.

In March 2015, Guinean health minister Remy Lamah, commenting on a new health-emergency declaration that was about to go into effect, told us:

> The epidemic has reached the coastal zone. This is due to several factors. Many people deny the existence of the disease. There are false rumors. There is misinformation in some communities. People are not complying with certain measures decreed by the health services, or with those involving the transfer of bodies from one place to another, contact control, and unsafe burial practices.

Guinea's minister of communications, Alhousseine Makanera Kaké, worked diligently on a new project to raise awareness, which he joined through his regular visits to communities:

> Each community chooses fifteen young people and fifteen women, and we take them to the treatment center so they can see how the work is done there, including the handling of the bodies of the deceased. In some communities we've asked that they dress like health workers and really see what happens from that perspective and then be able to dispel the misinformation, the rumors that make people believe it was the government that imported the disease, that white people have come to kill Guineans.
>
> We organize discussions through the radio, linking together public and community radio stations—two in Conakry and twenty-eight in other parts of the country. In this way, a person at one end of the country can talk to someone at the other end. Someone in Conakry can talk

to someone in the border area and exchange experiences, talk about the situation in their respective communities. This allows the people to understand that what is happening in their community is also happening in others.

We've been able to humanize the treatment centers. At first they were like prisons. After a person was admitted no one saw them, and more often than not, they left the facility as a corpse. But today, in centers such as Coyah, you can see the patients and talk with them, and that has reassured the population. When I visit the interior of the country, 90 percent of the time I communicate with people in the various national [indigenous] languages.

Two songs, two perspectives

Good intentions are undone by ignorance and arrogance. Not on the part of unschooled or illiterate Africans, but of Europeans and Americans who—ignorant of other worlds but eager to help—act superior and believe their world is *the* world.

In November 2014 renowned musicians Bob Geldof, U2's Bono, and Robert Plant of Led Zeppelin, among others, came together to record a song of "solidarity" with those afflicted with Ebola. But they didn't make the slightest effort to find out anything about the culture of the nations gripped by the epidemic. They assumed that what Londoners, Parisians, or New Yorkers believe, enjoy, and dream of is what the residents of Monrovia, Freetown, and Conakry long for.

The song's title "Do They Know It's Christmas?" was a disaster in terms of connecting with a population that is majority Muslim in two of the three affected countries. The lyrics, far from being educational, inaccurately described the epidemic and instilled fear among Europeans. It was actually a new version of an old song that Geldof had recorded 30 years ago to raise funds in response to the famine in Ethiopia. In Africa the song was widely condemned. A November 14, 2014, article by BBC World News reported the following response:

> "The vast majority of the population in Sierra Leone is Muslim. The vast majority of the population in Guinea is Muslim. So to ask us whether or not we know it's Christmas—yes, we know it's Christmas, but not all of us celebrate Christmas," said Robtel Neajai Pailey, a Liberian researcher at the University of London's School of Oriental and African Studies.
>
> Pailey said the song is not only "insulting" but unoriginal and it "reinforces stereotypes. . . . The lyrics have references to 'them' versus 'us,' and I think that's incredibly patronizing and problematic. So that's why I object to the lyrics."

As is often the case, Western celebrities dominated coverage in the Western media, pushing aside famous African artists such as Salif Keita, Amadou & Mariam, and Tiken Jah Fakoly, one of the greatest reggae artists on that continent. These musicians had previously written and released another song, with an educational purpose, titled "Africa Stop Ebola." It proved very popular. It immediately became a hashtag and won a following on the internet. These are some of the lyrics:

Africa Stop Ebola

Africa is full of sadness
To see our families die

Do not touch the sick
Do not touch the bodies
Everyone is in danger
Young and old
We must act for our families

Ebola, Ebola
Invisible enemy
(repeat chorus)

Ebola, you are our enemy
If you feel sick the doctors will help you
I assure you, the doctors will help you
There is hope to stop Ebola
Have confidence in the doctors

Ebola, Ebola
Trust the doctors
(repeat chorus)

Ebola is not good
You should see a doctor
(repeat chorus)

[. . .]

Again we talk about tragedy
As a false note in the melody
Ebola, we thought you were since abolished
You are walking around spreading disease
We will not flee from you, we will not hide
Because we know we have the means to
    push you away
We will strike you, we are not a plague
We will get together
We will beat you. . . .

Another tragedy strikes the continent
Africa needs vaccine, medicine
Is hope for them permitted?
Should we close our eyes and leave them in
    oblivion? (No!)
Then unite for a good cause
Mobilize and break the closed doors,
Ebola, I swear we will evict you
Africa needs vaccine and treatment

Ebola, Ebola
Trust the doctors
(repeat chorus)

Ebola: Doubts and certainties

Over time, I began to discern another aspect to the response given to us by Abigail, the Liberian teenager we had interviewed in a public school. It was probably the result of discussions among students and the parents who read more broadly. Some articles in the international alternative media—both the serious and the most sensationalist press—speculated on the most sundry and sometimes frightful hypotheses regarding the origin of the epidemic.

Perhaps Abigail and her father had read an article by Dr. Cyril Broderick, a former professor of plant pathology at the University of Liberia, in *Images: Liberian Societal, Lifestyle, Political Analysis & Business Magazine*, issue 14 in 2014. It's an attractively printed English-language publication sold for $5, a prohibitive price for many Liberians. Broderick was indignant at the official assessment of the epidemic's origin:

> About a week ago, I read an article published in the Internet news summary publication of the Friends of Liberia

that said that there was an agreement that the initiation of the Ebola outbreak in West Africa was due to the contact of a two-year-old child with bats that had flown in from the Congo. That report made me disconcerted with the reporting about Ebola, and it stimulated a response to the "Friends of Liberia," saying that African people are not ignorant and gullible, as is being implicated.

The author cited a 1998 book quoting a discussion between two US researchers who alleged a medical industry run by the military was conducting biological weapons tests in Africa. Broderick even claimed the existence of an experiment, launched in 2014, in which healthy Africans were injected with the Ebola virus—supposedly a million-dollar agreement with Tekmira, a Canadian pharmaceutical company. Beyond quotes from other articles and some plausible deductions, however, he offered no evidence.

Mohamed Touré—the son of Ahmed Sékou Touré, father of Guinean independence—slipped in an insinuation of suspicion when we interviewed him at his home in Conakry: "It's not really known how it [Ebola] emerged, but eventually history will tell us." He said nothing more.

Historical evidence does exist that biological weapons have been used in armed conflicts or destabilization efforts in various countries at different times. There is abundant documentation of how US forces used Agent Orange in Vietnam, as well as how chemical or biological agents have repeatedly been introduced into Cuba to kill crops, livestock, and humans.

In the case of Cuba, initial speculation was subsequently confirmed with the declassification of documentary evidence. In a June 2, 2015, article in *Granma*, Pedro Etcheverry Vázquez reported on the history of attacks targeting public health and food sources in Cuba, under the pointed headline: "Impossible to forget biological attacks." It noted that during the 1970s and '80s, US intelligence agencies introduced into the island "hemorrhagic conjunctivitis, dysentery, and dengue serotype 2, which killed 158 people, including 101 children—the greatest damage inflicted on our people by this kind of aggression."

We can add that the US government has waged a war against the Cuban Revolution, both open and undeclared, for more than fifty years, and that the war against Vietnam was one of the most shameful episodes of the twentieth century.

In the case of Ebola, however, it cannot be argued that the situation facing the three West African countries infected with Ebola was due to hostile relations with other countries.

Some authors engage in speculation and offer a host of seemingly plausible reasons for the spread of infectious agents, including accidents or human error, although some are so macabre that they tend not to be credible. These range from purely military intentions, whether aggressive or defensive, to birth control schemes, including plans to depopulate en masse large areas of the planet (what US president George W. Bush in a 2002 speech called "dark corners of the earth"). One such claim is that in 1982–87 apartheid South Africa had a biological weapons program designed to kill or sterilize the black population.

Others point to the interests of pharmaceutical companies, which they say have historically been allied with the military industry. These companies allegedly produce "hot" viruses as well as their cure, which can then be sold in mass quantities. If a virus or a disease doesn't threaten those with money to pay for the cure, then research projects on these subjects don't receive funding.

An epidemic such as the one in West Africa, with its

rapidly expanding death toll, often forces WHO to accept drugs in an experimental phase, without the prior testing that is normally required. That means large pharmaceutical corporations can reap results in one year that normally would take many years of preliminary testing.

Adame Cerón writes that there was a dispute between WHO and Doctors Without Borders—which according to him is favorable toward transnational pharmaceutical companies—around what the latter considered a belated declaration of an international health emergency. (Adame Cerón, pp. 202–3)

Cuban scientist Jorge Pérez Ávila, however, insists the procedure was rigorous and, in such situations, necessary:

> The protocols were well-defined. They were certified by ethics committees, because it was WHO, not the pharmaceutical companies, that did this. Animal testing was skipped—it went directly to human testing. There was pressure to solve the problem. And this led to the vaccine, which incidentally is effective.
>
> It's a US vaccine, which was developed together with the British and Canadians. I don't know to what extent it's used now, but ideally everyone in the infected regions should be vaccinated. As far as I know, there are two experimental vaccines that have given satisfactory results. So has the medicine.
>
> Steps were skipped, but it was an emergency. Maybe tomorrow they'll discover the medicine is carcinogenic— they didn't do studies for that. But it saved many lives, didn't it? How many times have we used a medicine for years that later was proven to have harmful side effects?

In fact, when Cuban volunteer Félix Báez became sick with Ebola, he was treated in Geneva with two experimental drugs that were at an advanced stage of clinical trials, ZMapp and Favipiravir. According to Dr. Jorge Pérez Ávila, who observed the patient's evolution from the time he was admitted, Favipiravir had an observable effect on him. Perhaps one of those drugs saved his life, or perhaps both, or neither.

To this can be added the suspicion that Africa has been and continues to be used as an experimental lab, and that both Africans and Latin Americans have been used as guinea pigs. There is also declassified evidence to support this. For example, in 2010 the White House publicly acknowledged that in 1946–48 US government researchers, in experiments testing the then-new drug penicillin, deliberately infected 696 Guatemalans with syphilis.[1]

Other authors point to a military laboratory in Fort Detrick, Maryland, that was known until 1969 as a center for the US biological weapons program. Today Fort Detrick houses the US Army Medical Research Institute for Infectious Diseases, which its website describes as "the Department of Defense's lead laboratory for medical biological defense research" to protect US military forces against anthrax, Ebola, and other biological agents. Incidentally, after World War II, Nazi scientist Erich Traub served as advisor to this laboratory.[2] But that's old news.

Documentaries, fictional films, and novels portraying Ebola and other rapidly spreading lethal viruses have set the tone for public perceptions of the Ebola epidemic. Fitting the Hollywood mold, they reinforce the Manichean view that the world is divided into good guys and bad guys, with the former always winning out.

---

1. Reuters, October 1, 2010.
2. *Washington Post*, February 22, 1998; Adame Cerón, p. 202.

Of course, there are "good guys" and "bad guys" within the US military itself. The argument that finally sways the less evil ones to reconsider their position, in the words of the general played by Morgan Freeman in the 1995 film *Outbreak* (based on the Robin Cook novel of the same name), is, "We have to defend ourselves against the other maniacs who are developing biological weapons."

These films follow the pattern set by the US media: the system is innocent—those to blame are obsessed or downright evil individuals or groups. But at least fiction acknowledges and prepares us to openly accept the possibility that the "bad guys" might take drastic action. In *Outbreak*, for example, they are about to drop a bomb that would wipe out the sick, the healthy, and the doctors at a mercenary camp in Zaire (Congo). And they give an order not to distribute a vaccine in time. A terrifying scene portrays the frantic exchange between the "good guys" (Dustin Hoffman and Cuba Gooding Jr.) as they rush to save 2,600 citizens who face being wiped out after an order is given to drop a fuel-air bomb on the infected community—which would vaporize everything within a mile radius—in order to keep the existence of the biological weapon secret.

"They want their weapon," says one. The other, taken aback, asks, "They'll kill everyone?" to which the first, who has understood the extent of Evil, replies, "Yes, they want their weapon."

American writer Richard Preston offers a different view in his 1994 bestselling novel *The Hot Zone* (with a 1998 translation to Spanish), which claims to be based on firsthand and scientific accounts. It portrays the discovery of the Marburg and Ebola viruses, the latter in its Zaire, Sudan, and Reston strains. Fort Detrick is described as a center for the control of infectious diseases and protection of public health. The book contains the following supposed exchange between the author and C. J. Peters, a doctor at the military facility, about the possibility of airborne transmission of the virus (subsequently ruled out):

> Looking back on the Reston event, he said to me one day that he was pretty sure Ebola had spread through the air. . . .
>
> "Did you ever try to see if you could put Ebola Reston into the air and spread it among monkeys that way?" I asked.
>
> "No," he replied firmly. "I just didn't think that was a good idea. If anybody had found out that the Army was doing experiments to see if the Ebola virus had adapted to spreading in the respiratory tract, we would have been accused of doing offensive biological warfare—trying to create a doomsday germ."[3]

Biological weapons certainly exist, along with those who produce them. Border detection of human or animal carriers of an infection and a country's response capability are matters of national security. Because there are those—as we noted at the beginning of this chapter—who speculate that the virus will be introduced into a country, whether accidentally or not, measures to prevent this are vital to the country's security.

Detected in 1976, the first Ebola outbreaks in humans were scattered and limited to remote, sparsely populated areas. The more serious cases of contagion occurred when a patient or patients arrived at hospitals that were unprepared and lacked resources. The first victims were among the medical personnel.

---

3. Richard Preston, *The Hot Zone*, (New York: Random House, 1994).

One of the first hospitals to treat patients infected with the virus at the beginning of the 2014–15 crisis was the facility in Kenema, Sierra Leone, near the border with Guinea and Liberia. I could go into all the speculation that has swirled around a US biomedical lab (subsequently dismantled), sponsored by Tulane University and the Fort Detrick laboratory, that was housed in the Kenema hospital. Broderick called it "a viral fever bioterrorism research laboratory," and associated it with the experiments he claimed were being conducted.

To the delight of fans of detective stories and conspiracy theories (always making conjectures that foster confusion and false leads rather than the truth), Glenn Thomas, a WHO expert on AIDS and Ebola working as a researcher at that lab, was on the Malaysia Airlines flight that was shot down over Ukraine in July 2014. Broderick, not doubting for a minute that the Kenema laboratory was responsible, asked in his article, "Are there others? Wherever they exist, it is time to terminate them."

Dr. Jorge Pérez Ávila, director of the Pedro Kourí Institute in Havana, however, stood by the official version, while noting the potential military uses of the virus:

> It's been documented that the outbreak originated in Guinea, not Kenema [Sierra Leone]. I don't doubt that there was a US laboratory there. This is a Level 4 virus, a biological warfare virus due to its capacity to kill—if I touch you, you're infected. It's a very contagious virus. It's a virus that could be used in biological warfare. You take a sample from a culture of that virus, you spread it, and it immediately sets off a chain of infection.
>
> I don't deny there might have been a laboratory there, but this didn't start in Kenema. It started in Guinea, from the very first case. It started because the necessary mea-

sures were not taken, and the infectious chain began when those infected traveled to the cities. There was no way to stop that. That's the scientific part.

The Americans, the British, and the French have also been working on this virus, because they know it has existed since the 1970s and is very aggressive. They've conducted experimental work, under the highest safety conditions, and have searched for a vaccine.

As far as I know, there has been no release of the virus, whether in Atlanta or Fort Detrick. This is a virus that because of its genetic structure—from my modest knowledge—cannot be invented. It lends itself to be manipulated, but I have no evidence of that.

In Kenema, more than forty Sierra Leonean nurses and doctors who were unprotected died suddenly with the outbreak of Ebola. The Atlanta CDC immediately established an Ebola Treatment Unit at that hospital.

Initially the Cuban medical brigade was going to be assigned to the Kenema center. Sierra Leone's government made a shift, however, after the decline in cases in that district and the increased incidence in Port Loko.

Enforcing US economic sanctions against Cuba, however, the US Treasury Department's Office of Foreign Assets Control (OFAC) obstructed Cuban health workers in Sierra Leone from receiving funds that WHO had allocated them to cover hotels, food, etc. That did not happen in Liberia or Guinea.

The Cuban brigade that went to Sierra Leone was the largest and first on the scene, and it found all the active players unprepared and unable to respond effectively. That delayed the Cubans' ability to join the battle against Ebola for a month and a half.

But Ebola's natural course and the official literature lead

us into the depths of the tropical jungle. Spanish scientist Rafael Delgado of the 12 de Octubre University Hospital, in Madrid, wrote:

> What is the origin of the Ebola virus (EV)? We don't fully know the ecology of the EV, but varieties of bats have been identified in Africa that could be a reservoir for the virus in the wild. From bats, the virus could infect other mammals such as antelopes and monkeys, which could infect humans through the consumption of wild animals.[4]

Cuban scientist Jorge Pérez Ávila reiterates that explanation:

> This is a disease that emerged at that time from an animal reservoir, in this case from a fruit-eating bat that inhabits the jungle and mostly infects monkeys, dogs, and pigs. Monkeys and dogs multiply the spread of the virus, coming into direct contact with humans. That's how transmission of the disease begins.

The above-mentioned novel by Richard Preston, written early on, notes that one route for the spread of AIDS and Ebola was Kinshasa Highway, "a transcontinental road that wanders across Africa from east to west and passes along the shores of Lake Victoria within sight of Mount Elgon . . . a huge, solitary extinct volcano that rises to a height of fourteen thousand feet near the edge of the Great Rift Valley" on the Uganda-Kenya border. Paved in the 1970s, it was a modern road that allowed passengers, traders, and hunters to travel to the most remote areas of

---

4. Dr. Rafael Delgado, December 2014 issue of the journal of the Spanish Society for Biochemistry and Molecular Biology (SEBBM).

Mount Elgon, where the first humans, to our knowledge, contracted the Marburg and Ebola viruses. The Ebola River intersects with the Congo River and is crossed by the Kinshasa Highway at various points. In the movie *Outbreak*, when US researchers inquire about "patient zero" in a small village in Zaire, they are told it was a man working on the construction of a road to Kinshasa.

Global communications would take care of the rest. An airplane, says Preston, becomes a biological missile if it carries even one infected passenger aboard. Every contact between a symptomatic individual and other passengers will spread the virus to the most unexpected and distant places. On arrival at the airport, that missile will explode in all directions. WHO projected an exponential increase in the number of people becoming infected. As Dr. Jorge Delgado told me:

> WHO had given a sensationalist estimate: by the end of October there would be 10,000 Ebola cases weekly in Sierra Leone. Ten thousand! The actual figure is 80 or 100 cases a week. Those are their figures, although there are people who were born and died in their communities that no one ever heard about. Nobody ever knew they existed. The government is making enormous efforts to reach these areas, and so is WHO.

They weren't the only ones. "According to statements by the US Centers for Disease Control and Prevention (CDC)," wrote Adame Cerón, "1,400,000 people could be affected by the 'deadly' Ebola virus by January 2015" (p. 188).

Fortunately, the predictions were wrong. The number of infections never surpassed 500 a week, which was still very high (and much higher than previous outbreaks). This was true despite the fact that, after the initial terror subsided and the number of patients decreased, taxis, other public transportation, and markets in the three capitals remained jammed with people in unrestricted contact with each other.

Preston's final thesis is attractive for those who view things in terms of abstract environmentalism, ignoring the capitalist character of "developmentalist" policies, which are deemed productive and "civilizing." It's true that unrestricted action by humans over nature may foster the deadly spread of so-called hot viruses previously confined to isolated jungle areas. But it's capitalism, with its un-quenchable thirst for profits, not "civilization," that skews the relationship between humans and nature.

"AIDS is the revenge of the rain forest. It is only the first act of the revenge," Preston writes. For him, the spread of the disease is "civilization's fault," because that virus, like many others, thrives in the jungle and is part of it, part of that amoral set of relations that is nature and its denizens, animals and (equally "savage") humans—a system that becomes "malignant" under the impact of the predatory actions of modern society.

It's the same thesis suggested by the film *Outbreak*, where a character says of the witch doctor in a village an-nihilated by the disease, "He believes that the gods were awoken from their sleep by men cutting down the trees, where no man should be. And the gods got angry. This is a punishment."

It's true that modern society has "contaminated" the African continent, but not because of the emergence of new technology and means of communication, which are both necessary and welcome. Today, for example, the urban populations of Conakry, Freetown, and Monrovia, the capitals of the three affected countries, use cellular telephones on a mass scale. Such a technological "leap" is necessary because of the historic absence of landline telephone systems in the region. Similarly, if a person of average means in those cities is able today to buy a laptop, it's because such a technological "leap" skipped over several generations of desktop computers that were never available.

Modern society has not left Africa behind—the African continent was a major actor in the founding of modern society, only on the grimmer side of that history. It provided slaves, raw materials, and cultures that were uprooted and then reborn in distant lands. These roots survived the long journey through space and time and sprouted outside their original environment. Africa contributed to the birth of modern society its own lack of development.

In his unpublished memoirs, Oscar Oramas, Cuban ambassador to Guinea and Mali from 1966 to 1974, recalled the "guidance" he received from Halidou Touré (not related to Sékou Touré), a senior official in Mali's foreign ministry. It was similar, the author noted, to what he had been told by leaders of the anticolonial movement such as Amilcar Cabral of Guinea-Bissau and Djibo Bakary of Niger:

> Things on the African continent have a long history. The first thing you have to study is the tribes, the great empires that emerged from them. You have to study the specter of colonization and its negative impact on the socioeconomic structure of societies. When the colonizers arrived, there was already development and culture here. And all those values were subverted or destroyed, and that is at the root of our ills today.
>
> European Marxists miss the nuances when attempting to analyze our realities, because they apply schemas

that conform to their own societies. Not only did Frantz Fanon say this, but these are historical truths. People who for centuries lived under colonialism cannot act, think, and possess the reflexes of people who have lived another kind of life. . . . Here human beings have other motivations, other needs to satisfy. Social changes should not and cannot be made without taking these factors into account. Otherwise they lead to failure.

Now, let's place these factors in their proper order. All these irrational reasons may or may not have contributed to the epidemic, but its spread is the result, first and foremost, of inherited poverty. The number one vector causing and transmitting fatal diseases is poverty, with all its social and cultural consequences. And poverty in Africa is the daughter of modern society, that is, capitalism. Capitalism engenders poverty, biological warfare, the profit drive, and ecological catastrophes.

In his incisive study, Miguel Ángel Adame Cerón asks virus researchers to examine society in this region:

> Since the vast majority of cases have occurred in the region of Central Africa and now West Africa . . . we must not limit our search to which kind of harmful microorganism is involved. We must also look for the specific kind of organisms Ebola has attacked: what is the degree of strength, vitality, nutrition, attitude—in short, overall equilibrium—of the human beings who are susceptible to this hemorrhagic disease.
>
> What has been found, of course, is that the people where the worst outbreaks of this epidemic have occurred live in a veritable state of pauperism. They also share a biological, ecological, and socioeconomic vulnerability (although the state of their immune systems has received little attention).

And this is all a product of capitalist McGlobalization, which sharply polarizes conditions between a wealthy minority and a majority that lives in extreme poverty. (p. 76)

Cuban doctors and nurses did not go to that region to determine the origin of the epidemic. They went there to save lives. Nonetheless, Dr. Jorge Delgado, head of the Cuban brigade in Sierra Leone, was completely clear in his response:

> Why Ebola? Because Ebola threatens the big powers. Ebola is a disease of poverty—of poverty in the strictest and purest sense—just as malaria is a disease of poverty, along with pneumonia, meningitis, and all other infectious diseases associated with malnutrition. The number of cases, in fact, is minimal compared to, say, malaria.
>
> Let's take the pediatric ward here. In the last few days, twelve or thirteen children were admitted. None tested positive for Ebola. What did they test positive for? Pneumonia, cerebral malaria, gastroenteritis, meningitis, malnutrition with sepsis of various kinds—all associated with poverty.
>
> I can't give you the actual number of malaria cases, but a lot of people will continue to die, even though there are relatively easy ways to prevent the disease. In this area we face a problem with malaria. Tuberculosis is a problem. AIDS is a problem. I can't tell you whether 30 or 40 percent of the population is HIV-positive as it was in Zimbabwe, or whether it's 15 or 20 percent. But it must be high, because habits such as promiscuity and lack of protection are widespread, as they have been in the case of Ebola.
>
> I once spoke with Ban Ki-moon's representative during a meeting at the Radisson Hotel in Freetown (he was a Spaniard and was very happy to be able to speak in

Spanish, since he hadn't been with Spanish-speakers in a long time). I told him, "Look, this is the country of the 70 percent: 70 percent are hungry, 70 percent aren't working, don't have jobs, don't have money, can't read or write, don't have radios, don't have TVs, don't have access to the press—they're disconnected from the world. If seven out of ten people are in bad shape, you can't do much with the other three. Sierra Leone is the country of the 70 percent, the second poorest in the world."

When a patient suspected of having Ebola is treated in an African center set up for such purposes, sophisticated laboratory techniques are used to confirm whether the person has contracted the virus or has malaria; other diseases are not tested for. These lab operations are installed and almost exclusively run by European and US technicians, who are usually reluctant to have journalists present.

In other words, Ebola mortality statistics don't take into account two essential facts. One is whether the patient has another underlying disease, such as AIDS or tuberculosis, or whether the person suffers from malnutrition. The other is the stage of evolution of the disease—for example, whether the patient was admitted five days or more after the onset of symptoms. In both cases the outcome will almost certainly be death. These two facts, of course, distort any statistical measure of the real mortality rate.

That's why Dr. Rotceh Ríos Molina, head of the Cuban medical team at the Waterloo ADRA Ebola Treatment Unit in Sierra Leone, noted:

> When we arrived October 9 and entered an Ebola ward, it looked like a warehouse for the sick, not a hospital. Many people were lying on the floor. They hadn't been fitted with IVs. They weren't being given medication. So we

had to alter the notion that they couldn't be touched. We began to treat them, and more patients began to survive. The deadliness of the disease resulted from the lack of treatment.

WHO established a protocol that we observed, although with a few small modifications. Enteral (oral) and parenteral (intravenous) hydration. Antimalarial drugs as a preventive measure—everyone there has the malaria parasite. Antibiotics to prevent superinfection. General measures: duralgin, paracetamol [acetaminophen] to reduce fever, and a coagulant to stop bleeding. That's what we did.

Now, there were some patients we suspected had tuberculosis, for example, and we tried to treat them for that. Or pneumonia, and in addition to Rocephin we gave them theophylline to reinforce it. Then we began to make discrete modifications to that protocol, with the aim of treating the diseases they brought with them, because everyone arrived sick with something, plus Ebola. So we tried to cure them of that as well as treat them for Ebola.

Dr. Graciliano Díaz Bartolo, who headed the Comprehensive Health Program and later served as deputy head of the brigade in Guinea fighting Ebola, noted:

There are no statistics, no figures. It's hard to speak of the health situation in the country—there is no health awareness at any level. And that has allowed the disease to spread, at home and abroad. Right now we're talking about Ebola, but before that it was malaria, meningoencephalitis, cholera, typhoid fever, tuberculosis, AIDS. And the country's health department doesn't know what the current situation is regarding these diseases. It has given up monitoring them. And once the fight against Ebola ends, it will have to resume that work.

Malaria has cost the lives of thousands of Guineans. Many have suffered serious consequences from it such as liver and brain damage. But Ebola is the most lethal thing we've seen, because it's an enemy that can be found anywhere.

Health indicators for the three countries are not accurate but are still revealing. I'll just mention some data from a report the Cuban health ministry prepared for the doctors and nurses going to those countries.

In Liberia the infant mortality rate is 56 per 1,000 live births (in Cuba it's 4.2). Maternal mortality per 100,000 live births is 990 (44 in Cuba[5]). The prevalence of HIV/AIDS and of tuberculosis is 521 and 495 per 100,000 inhabitants, respectively. Yet Liberia has only 0.1 doctor per 10,000 inhabitants.

In Sierra Leone the figures are even starker. Infant mortality is 117 per 1,000 live births; maternal mortality is 860 per 100,000 live births. There are 965 cases of HIV/AIDS and 1,304 of tuberculosis for every 100,000 inhabitants. There is an average of 0.2 doctors per 10,000 Sierra Leoneans.

And in Guinea, infant mortality is 65 per 1,000 live births and maternal mortality is 980 per 100,000 live births. Of every 100,000 Guineans, 1,031 suffer from HIV/AIDS and 274 from tuberculosis (data published by the Cuban health ministry). The number of doctors in the country is not recorded, although Guinea has a cadre of doctors who were trained in Cuba going back to the early 1960s.

---

5. Cuba's overall maternal mortality rate in 2018 was 44 per 100,000 live births; direct maternal mortality—due to complications in childbirth—was 27.5 per 100,000 live births (figures provided by Cuba's health ministry).

Adame Cerón presents additional figures provided by the United Nations Development Program: out of 187 countries on its Human Development Index for 2014, Liberia, Guinea, and Sierra Leone rank number 175, 179, and 183, respectively. The rate of extreme poverty is 65 percent in Liberia, 55 percent in Guinea, and 53 percent in Sierra Leone.

When the Ebola epidemic broke out in Guinea and Sierra Leone, Cuban medical brigades had already been working in those countries as part of the Comprehensive Health Program. Jorge Lefebre, Cuba's ambassador to those two countries and resident in Accra, Ghana, told me about the arrival of that initial brigade in Sierra Leone in 2011:

> Just as we were introducing the Comprehensive Health Program brigade to the government, the health minister at that time said something I'll never forget:
> "You cannot imagine how much we appreciate this medical aid that Cuba is giving us. In countries around the world, when a woman becomes pregnant, it is cause for happiness in the family. In my country it is cause for deep sadness. It means that at the end of pregnancy, one of the two will die—the mother or the child. You are going to help us so that no longer happens."

'Dad, be strong—everything is going to be fine'

On November 18, 2014, a news release issued by the Cuba's health ministry shocked the nation:

> On November 16, Dr. Félix Báez Sarría, an internal-medicine specialist who had treated Ebola patients in Sierra Leone as part of the brigade in the Henry Reeve International Contingent that is fighting the epidemic, developed a fever of 38–39 degrees [Celsius, or 102–104 degrees Fahrenheit]; otherwise he had no symptoms. He was immediately transferred to the Kerry Town Ebola Treatment Unit in the capital [Freetown], which is designated for treating UN officials, and where Cuban professionals work.
>
> On November 17 he was given an Ebola diagnostic test that was positive. Our health worker is being cared for by a team of British professionals who have experience treating patients with this disease. They remain in regular communication with doctors in our brigade.
>
> At the suggestion of the World Health Organization, it

was decided to transfer Dr. Félix Báez Sarría to the University Hospital in Geneva, Switzerland, since this is a specialized center with experience in treating and managing highly contagious infections.

Specialists and officials continue to follow the patient's progress. So far he has had no complications and has stable blood circulation.

Ministry of Public Health

Everyone's worst fears had come true. In the early days of the brigade's work, two Cuban doctors had gone out wearing their special "space" suits after a day of intense activity—working longer hours than recommended—to pick up a dying Ebola patient that an ambulance crew had thrown into the gutter, like a useless sack, just a few meters from the Kerry Town center. It's not certain but assumed that the contact occurred then. Not even Félix can pinpoint when or how it happened.

A few days later he came down with a fever. Doctors Luis Escalona and Felipe Delgado had physical contact with him in Port Loko, a few hours after the first symptoms appeared. They were subjected to a rigorous quarantine.

Escalona feels a chill when he recalls the dream Félix had about a snake. Félix woke up with fever and sweats. "I dreamed of a huge boa squeezing me," he told his colleague. "It opened its mouth wide and was trying to swallow me, and you saved me." Death was lurking.

The odds seemed to be leaning toward the worst predictions of the enemy press. They were hoping that Cubans, worried about their relatives, friends, and fellow citizens, would come to resent the sending of the medical brigades. But that didn't happen. The news didn't discourage but rather broadened the solidarity: all Cubans felt part of

Felix's family. A brief, moving message posted by his son on Cuban news websites set off an explosion of deep feelings throughout the country:

> Hi, I'm Félix's son. My name is Alejandro. I want to thank all those who in one way or another are giving encouragement and hope to our family and to my father. I also want to acknowledge the health authorities who made it possible for my father to start getting medical care so soon and be transferred to Geneva to be cared for with all means available. I know everything will turn out all right, and in a few months it will be just a story to tell.
>
> To those still there, doing their beautiful work in spite of the risks, courage! And thanks for taking care of my dad while I'm not with him. All our hopes are with you. Greetings to all.
>
> Dad, be strong—everything is going to be fine. Over here, all of Cuba is pulling for you.

Those Cuban news sites received hundreds of messages. The decision to go fight Ebola had been seen as heroic from the beginning, but now the real possibility of death made it even more so in the public's imagination. Despite the pragmatism that seemed to prevail in the social climate of the new century, it was confirmed once again that heroes are not a thing of the past. People anxiously awaited news and counted every day of life that went by as a victory. The news was promising. Alejandro Báez, Félix's son, sent a new message:

> Thank you for helping my comments reach out so that everyone could support the cause of our doctors in Africa. That's what they need the most after this. Let's show our appreciation for what they're doing despite the hazards of

their work. That's the best way to make them feel safe and give them encouragement to keep moving forward with such an important mission.

Yes, my father got sick, but that doesn't mean, as many say, that he shouldn't have gone. I say it's just the opposite. My father was over there putting his life on the line because he felt it was his duty to help those who needed it the most. But I say: isn't that what makes us human? What makes us human is our ability to put the common good above personal considerations, to give our all to help those who need a hand.

I take this opportunity to again thank everyone for showing so much support and love toward our medical volunteers, especially toward my father.

From their prisons in the United States, Gerardo Hernández, Tony Guerrero, and Ramón Labañino anxiously followed news of Félix's health.[1] Gerardo wrote to Dr. Rotceh Ríos Molina, a fellow resident of Jaruco (a town east of Havana) now in Sierra Leone.

Dear brother Rotceh:

I was able to read the note you wrote to Marlene [Caboverde, a Radio Jaruco reporter who had put them in touch]. I thank you for your words, and I'm glad to have this opportunity to send you greetings. Ever since we heard the news about the departure of Cuban medical brigades for West Africa to fight the Ebola epidemic, we've tried to stay abreast of the extraordinary work our compatriots have been doing.

We've recently been paying special attention to the condition of Dr. Félix Báez, who fortunately seems to be making satisfactory progress. I don't think there is a more

1. See footnote on the Cuban Five, p. 121.

direct way for me to communicate with him, so I'm taking advantage of this message to convey our best wishes to Félix for his prompt and full recovery.

On more than a few occasions over the years, the Five have been asked what inspires us to resist this unjust imprisonment for so long, so far from Cuba and our families. Even before the current Ebola crisis, we always talked about the conduct of the Cuban doctors and other internationalists as an important source of encouragement, pride, and inspiration for us.

Now, with this extraordinary lesson in heroism you're giving the world, we feel even prouder, and there are no words to express how much you fortify us by your example. Today you are our heroes! To all the compañeras and compañeros who are part of the Cuban medical brigades in West Africa, we express our immense admiration and ask you to take good care of yourselves. I know some day, when you've won that battle for the benefit of humanity, and when justice has been won for the Five, we'll have the opportunity to greet each other in our country. We wish you success, brothers!

Ever onward to victory!

Gerardo Hernández Nordelo
US Penitentiary, Victorville, California
November 21, 2014

Meanwhile, in a letter written just ten days before the remaining three of the Five were released from US prisons, Tony Guerrero told Félix of his immense joy on learning that he had finally recovered.

Dear Dr. Félix Báez, brother,
   Sometimes you receive news that fills you with immense joy and indescribable strength.

I was convinced you would defeat Ebola with your own strength and with all the medical care and solidarity surrounding you.

When I read the news about your return home, I felt tremendous happiness.

When I also read that from the beginning you said, and have now reiterated, that you are "going back to Sierra Leone to finish what you started," my heart was filled with an invincible resistance and immense pride in being Cuban.

It reminds me of when I was fortunate to attend the sentencing hearings for my brothers and I saw them give their statements before a judge we knew would give us the harshest and most unjust sentences. Without fear, full of conviction and high spirits, they said they were ready to go back and do everything they had done before to stop terrorist acts against our noble people.

Here your example remains firm, certain of victory.

Five strong embraces.

Antonio Guerrero Rodríguez
Marianna Federal Correctional Institution
December 7, 2014

Geneva

Dr. Jorge Pérez Ávila, director of Havana's Pedro Kourí Institute, was an exceptional witness to Félix's recovery in Geneva:

When I received the news I didn't pay attention to the name—I knew it was a volunteer. Someone said "Felito" but nothing more. I went home and commented that it seemed there was a volunteer over there with a fever, and they were

"The Five have been asked what inspires us to resist our unjust imprisonment. Cuban internationalist doctors have been an encouragement and a source of pride. Your example strengthens us."　—Gerardo Hernández writing from US prison to a Cuban doctor in Sierra Leone November 2014

RAMÓN ESPINOSA/AP

Havana, December 2014. Five Cuban revolutionaries at celebration of release of final three from US prisons a few days earlier. The five had been imprisoned for up to 16 years because of their actions defending Cuba from US-backed attacks. Cuban internationalist solidarity in the fight against Ebola epidemic in West Africa gave powerful boost to worldwide campaign demanding that Washington free the five Cuban heroes.

testing to determine what it was. And then someone in the house jumped up and said, "Damn, that must be Felito."

At that point it hit me that Felito was a relative of my wife, a cousin. It was Félix Báez. Of course I knew him. Until then I hadn't realized it was him.

Shortly afterward, maybe a few hours later, the minister called me and said, "Start packing—you're off to Geneva. Félix has tested positive, and you have to be on top of everything concerning his diagnosis and treatment. You'll join in and work at the hospital in Geneva. Ambassador Anayansi Rodríguez, Cuba's representative to the United Nations, and our embassy staff will help you." That night I boarded the plane.

Almost simultaneously, Dr. Félix Báez, now a patient, began the journey to Geneva. It seemed like it would never end. First, in an ambulance that just kept moving along with siren screaming, until they reached the city airport. Then, on a plane that was fully equipped for intensive care, which had to refuel for a several-hour flight. During the trip, they put him in the special suit used in the red zone. That's how he walked down the stairs off the plane, semiconscious and disoriented, held up by two doctors dressed like him. Félix didn't know where he was or who he was with. He had a high fever. They laid him on a stretcher and wrapped him in cellophane.

He was again put in an ambulance, this time escorted by two Geneva police cars, something very unusual in that city. They entered the hospital through an underground tunnel. Everything happened very quickly, synchronized, like the science fiction films. They took him out of the ambulance, assisted by security agents who were also protected with special suits, although they were nervous— it was the first Ebola case they had handled. Automatic doors opened, one after another, at the precise moment they passed through, until they reached the room where he would be staying, a so-called Biosafety Level 4 unit, fully equipped and in complete isolation.

When they undressed him under the sheets, he lay there just as he had traveled, as he had arrived at the hospital, as he had been born—completely naked—because Félix would now be reborn. His clothing had been incinerated in Sierra Leone. We can picture the entire scene. Félix didn't see it; he was unconscious.

Dr. Jorge Pérez was already at the hospital in Geneva. He had waited there all night together with Ambassador Anayansi Rodríguez. At that moment, no task was more important for the Cuban delegation, which has responsibilities on several United Nations commissions.

At 5:30 a.m. Dr. Jorge spoke with Dr. Jérôme Pugin, head of intensive care at the hospital. "He told me the patient was not well," Jorge said. "He remained unconscious with a high fever. He seemed to be suffering from some neurological complications. His transaminase and amylase levels were high. In other words, he had liver and pancreatic impairment, and was dehydrated." Jorge would stay with him from that point on.

For the first twelve hours Félix didn't recognize Jorge. Suddenly he noticed him on the other side of the glass and smiled. It was a familiar face, from back home. They communicated by phone through the glass that separated them. At times his coordination was off; Félix didn't notice it, but Dr. Jorge did.

During those first few hours of seeing each other again, Félix surprised Dr. Jorge—who thought he had seen it all—when he said, "Prof, I feel lousy, but I'm going to recover. And I'm going back to Sierra Leone."

"I was really moved," he told me, "because here was this man who was dying"—his face was swollen, his eyes a little

red—"and suddenly he says, 'I'm going back to Sierra Leone.'" Later he learned that before leaving Freetown, Félix
had told his co-workers the same thing.

Dr. Jorge was part of the discussions about the patient's
condition with the Swiss team that was treating him:

> He got very red, and the doctors started to think one of the
> medications was harming him. I told them, "No, that's a
> viral rash. Don't touch it or change the treatment." All the
> symptoms began to improve.
>
> But I wanted to know what Félix's viral load was. He
> had come in with a load of more than ten million copies
> of the virus per milliliter. Then it started to go down. I fol-
> lowed his condition clinically. We were able to continue
> with the medications, and there were no problems.
>
> Yes, we debated a lot how he was progressing. We no-
> ticed he had very high levels of a muscle enzyme called
> creatine phosphokinase, indicating he had muscular detri-
> tus, a significant loss of muscle tissue. The amylase, which
> like the transaminase was very high, began to go down
> and down. . . . Through the use of the medication and his
> own defenses, viral replication was reduced to the point
> where it was no longer detectable.
>
> That was around day fourteen—we were there for sev-
> enteen days. After seventy-two, maybe seventy-six hours
> of seeing this favorable change in his condition, I called in
> a report and said, "He's not going to die." You know why?
> The first thing Félix said to me was, "I'm hungry, I want to
> eat," even though he was in no position to eat. That's the
> best symptom he could have. The test results kept improv-
> ing and the viral load decreasing.

Dr. Jorge continued to follow these details and reported
daily to Cuba on the patient's recovery. Through the doc-

tors who were directly caring for Félix, Jorge sent messages to Félix's son that were published in the Cuban press. Months later, in Freetown, when the Cuban brigade members were already heading home, I met Félix Báez. It was the day before March 23, his forty-fourth birthday. After the necessary hug, he agreed to answer some questions. He told me:

> While I was in Geneva, around the fifth day of my hospitalization, Dr. Jérôme Pugin, head of intensive care at the University Hospital, told me about my son's message. One evening he brought it to me and I read it. It was very moving, I even cried. I didn't cry when I felt sick, but I cried when I read my son's letter. I have a lot of confidence in him, but I didn't expect such a beautiful selfless attitude.

When the viral load was no longer detectable, it became clear they had to leave the hospital and the city. The cost of his recovery, which WHO and the hospital itself were covering, was almost half a million dollars. "In Geneva Félix had been cared for by an excellent group of medical professionals," Dr. Jorge Pérez emphasized, "including Pugin, who established a great relationship with us and who loves Cuba."

Ambassador Anayansi Rodríguez bought Félix new clothes. With the help of the doctors, he was taken out through a hospital back door and given a quick tour of the city. Félix was coming back to life but was still frail. He tired easily; he couldn't walk very fast. That evening the Cuban embassy organized a welcome reception. The next day, Doctors Jorge Pérez Ávila and Félix Báez Sarría returned home to Cuba.

At that point it was still possible—and would be so for an unknown period—for the virus to be transmitted through his semen. Cuban television broadcast his arrival in Havana, with his wife and son waiting at the airport.

A month later he returned to Sierra Leone, as he had promised, but first he stopped in Geneva to donate blood—loaded with antibodies—to another Ebola patient who was being admitted to that hospital. Happily, by the time of his final return to Cuba, the semen tests had come out negative.

When we met in Freetown he also told me the following:

I heard about the support I've received in Cuba. When I was in Geneva I read an article titled, "Eleven million Cubans await you." There were lots of comments on [the online news sites] *Cubadebate* as well as *CubaSí*, and nearly eighty-five thousand hits on Twitter and Facebook. I heard about all this while I was in the hospital, and it was amazing.

I saw myself not as Félix but as just another Cuban who unfortunately was sick and was getting solidarity from an entire people and from around the world. I believe this helped raise some awareness in the world. It helped people learn that a Cuban medical brigade was fighting Ebola in Africa, and that it was necessary to extend aid to the people of Africa. I think it increased awareness among a lot of people.

Rejoining the mission was very positive. First, because I became an emblem of the brigade, a moral spearhead. It showed that people could be saved, that the Cuban Revolution would always support us, that no matter the costs, we would be well cared for.

I felt so moved when I returned to Sierra Leone. My co-workers all welcomed me with hugs, dozens and dozens of photos and hugs.

Previously I had been selected to be among the first

two hundred Cubans who would have traveled to New Orleans after Hurricane Katrina in 2005. I was a founding member of the Henry Reeve Contingent. I'm very proud to have been among the first to join and to have been present at the two most challenging moments for the contingent: Pakistan in 2005—one of the biggest earthquake disasters—and Sierra Leone today, the most serious epidemic. That's very important to me. Those have been my two missions.[2]

My wife helped me a lot. She supported me in everything. When I decided to go back to Sierra Leone, she told me it couldn't be any other way: that's the way I was, otherwise I wouldn't be her husband, and she supported and understood me.

---

2. For origin of Henry Reeve Contingent and response to Hurricane Katrina and Pakistan earthquake in 2005, see beginning of chapter "The Men I," under heading "Tracing the footsteps of the Henry Reeve Contingent."

David, Goliath, and other reflections

Nothing had suggested that December 17, 2014, would mark a historic milestone in international relations.[1] The news surprised those who were not part of the back-channel talks between Goliath and David—between the world's most powerful imperialist government and this rebellious island, an island-boat that, with uncommon faith in times of disbelief, kept sailing in search of Utopia and had not lowered its sails after the version of socialism carried out in European waters had sunk.

The talks were between two governments, or rather, two systems that had had no relations for more than half a century. At least formally, the two contenders were acknowl-

---

1. On December 17, 2014, Cuban president Raúl Castro and US president Barack Obama announced that diplomatic relations between the two countries, broken by Washington in 1961, would be reestablished. The same day, the US government released Gerardo Hernández, Ramón Labañino, and Antonio Guerrero, the last of the Cuban Five prisoners to be freed. See footnote on the Cuban Five on page 121.

edging and accepting each other on the basis of mutual respect. Goliath finally recognized the existence of David.

That afternoon (it was midday in Cuba), the Cuban volunteers in Guinea were at Le Rocher Hotel in Conakry, waiting for the opening of the Coyah Ebola Treatment Unit two days later. Meanwhile, Cuban doctors and nurses were following their work routines on different shifts at the treatment centers in Monrovia, Liberia, and at the Kerry Town and Maforki–Port Loko centers in Sierra Leone. Another group was on its way to the area of Waterloo, Sierra Leone, where a third center would open December 20. By then Dr. Félix Báez's life had been saved.

That day, Luis Escalona and other brigade members carried out the dangerous ritual they undertook every month: withdrawing funds from the local Freetown bank to pay for the brigade's housing, food, and stipends. Such transactions had initially been hampered by the US Treasury Department's Office of Foreign Assets Control. As Escalona told me:

> That day we had to withdraw money from the bank for the brigade in Sierra Leone. It was always one of the riskiest tasks we faced. There were a lot of weapons in that country. A civil war had ended there just 10 years before. There was extreme poverty. I'm not just talking about social indicators—the extreme poverty in Sierra Leone was palpable.
>
> And every month we had to go withdraw money from the bank. It was an ordeal because whenever we went into the bank, we didn't know when we'd leave. They might make us wait one hour or five hours, just to mess with us because we were Cuban. Because of the US blockade, Cuba could not appear on any list of dollar transactions. But we would be "sportsmanlike" and "take it easy," waiting in the area for customers withdrawing

large sums of money.

We were watching Al-Jazeera on TV. Suddenly there was an announcement that Raúl and Obama would both be speaking at the same time. That day it took us less time than usual at the bank; we quickly returned to the hotel. There we connected to Cubavisión Internacional online. That's how we were able to listen to Raúl's speech.

That morning in Cuba, a small group of writers was having an exchange with university students in the city of Camagüey. The writers had been invited by the Federation of University Students (FEU), which in December was celebrating its 82nd anniversary. One of the panelists, seated beside me, was writer and university professor Raúl Antonio Capote, a former Cuban state security agent who had worked undercover inside the CIA.

Capote was handed a note with a startling message. We were told not to publicize the news yet, but that in a few hours our president would announce in a speech that US agent Alan Gross had returned to his country and that the three Cuban antiterrorists still imprisoned in the United States were expected to be released immediately.

When that note passed before my eyes, I was overcome by emotion at the news; my voice wavered. It was 10:00 a.m. (3:00 p.m. in Conakry, Freetown and Monrovia) when we decided to share with the students what little we knew. There was an outburst of emotions—applause, cheers, tears, and hugs. The subject and tone of the meeting changed. Sketchy news reports trickled in. At noon (5:00 p.m. in West Africa) we were all gathered around the TV. President Raúl confirmed the rumors: the three heroes—Gerardo Hernández, Tony Guerrero, and Ramón Labañino—were now back in our country, after sixteen years of unjust imprisonment.

The emotional impact of this news was not surpassed by the second announcement—on the resumption of diplomatic relations between the Cuban and US governments. People took to the streets to celebrate the return of the three prisoners. But they were accustomed to years of living without the United States, and were mindful of the contradictory forces within the imperialist power that might end up derailing or reversing any good intentions.

The rapid Cuban response to the Ebola crisis in Africa, which took the US government by surprise, and the co-operation between Cuban and US doctors on African soil had an impact on international public opinion. On October 17, a few weeks after the arrival of the first brigade members from the Henry Reeve Contingent, US secretary of state John Kerry stated, "Now already we are seeing nations large and small stepping up in impressive ways to make a contribution on the frontlines. . . . Cuba, a country of just 11 million people, has sent 165 health professionals, and it plans to send nearly 300 more."

On October 18, in another article on Cuban participation in the fight against Ebola, Fidel wrote:

> We all understand that in carrying out this work with maximum preparation and efficiency, we will also be protecting our own people and our sister nations of Latin America and the Caribbean by preventing the spread of the virus, since it has unfortunately been introduced and could spread further in the United States, a country with many personal links and exchanges with the rest of the world.
>
> We will gladly cooperate with US personnel in this endeavor, not in pursuit of peace between these two states that have been adversaries for so many years, but of world peace, a goal that can and must be pursued.

Since becoming president, Barack Obama had received clear messages from his Latin American and Caribbean counterparts about the abusive, unjust, and futile nature of the US blockade against Cuba. These messages generally praised the solidarity extended by Cuba in the field of health care. In 2009, just months after the US president took office, those leaders gathered in Trinidad and Tobago for the Fifth Summit of the Americas, where they reiterated this message. Obama spoke at a subsequent press conference about the impact of what he called "Cuban medical diplomacy."

But it was in Haiti, after the deadly 2010 earthquake, that Cubans and Americans effectively collaborated for the first time in providing humanitarian aid. The US government's official policy, however, was at odds with its acknowledgment of these facts. In an editorial headlined, "A Cuban Brain Drain, Courtesy of the US," published almost exactly a month before December 17, the influential *New York Times* noted:

> Secretary of State John Kerry and the American ambassador to the United Nations, Samantha Power, have praised the work of Cuban doctors dispatched to treat Ebola patients in West Africa. The Centers for Disease Control and Prevention recently sent an official to a regional meeting the Cuban government convened in Havana to coordinate efforts to fight the disease. In Africa, Cuban doctors are working in American-built facilities. The epidemic has had the unexpected effect of injecting common sense into an unnecessarily poisonous relationship.
>
> And yet, Cuban doctors serving in West Africa today could easily abandon their posts, take a taxi to the nearest American Embassy and apply for a little-known immigration program that has allowed thousands of them to

defect. Those who are accepted can be on American soil within weeks, on track to becoming United States citizens.

There is much to criticize about Washington's failed policies toward Cuba and the embargo it has imposed on the island for decades. But the Cuban Medical Professional Parole Program, which in the last fiscal year enabled 1,278 Cubans to defect while on overseas assignments, a record number, is particularly hard to justify.

It is incongruous for the United States to value the contributions of Cuban doctors who are sent by their government to assist in international crises like the 2010 Haiti earthquake while working to subvert that government by making defection so easy.

American immigration policy should give priority to the world's neediest refugees and persecuted people. It should not be used to exacerbate the brain drain of an adversarial nation at a time when improved relations between the two countries are a worthwhile, realistic goal. (November 16, 2014)

Earlier, on October 19, the *New York Times* had taken up the subject from another angle, under an explicit headline, "Cuba's Impressive Role on Ebola":

Cuba is an impoverished island that remains largely cut off from the world and lies about 4,500 miles from the West African nations where Ebola is spreading at an alarming rate. Yet, having pledged to deploy hundreds of medical professionals to the front lines of the pandemic, Cuba stands to play the most robust role among the nations seeking to contain the virus. . . .

The global panic over Ebola has not brought forth an adequate response from the nations with the most to offer. While the United States and several other wealthy countries have been happy to pledge funds, only Cuba and a few nongovernmental organizations are offering what is most needed: medical professionals in the field. . . .

It is a shame that Washington, the chief donor in the fight against Ebola, is diplomatically estranged from Havana, the boldest contributor. In this case the schism has life-or-death consequences, because American and Cuban officials are not equipped to coordinate global efforts at a high level. This should serve as an urgent reminder to the Obama administration that the benefits of moving swiftly to restore diplomatic relations with Cuba far outweigh the drawbacks. . . .

Secretary of State John Kerry on Friday praised "the courage of any health care worker who is undertaking this challenge," and made a brief acknowledgment of Cuba's response. As a matter of good sense and compassion, the American military, which now has about 550 troops in West Africa, should commit to giving any sick Cuban access to the treatment center the Pentagon built in Monrovia and to assisting with evacuation.

The work of these Cuban medics benefits the entire global effort and should be recognized for that. But Obama administration officials have callously declined to say what, if any, support they would give them.

The Cuban health sector is aware of the risks of taking on dangerous missions. Cuban doctors assumed the lead role in treating cholera patients in the aftermath of Haiti's earthquake in 2010. Some returned home sick, and then the island had its first outbreak of cholera in a century. An outbreak of Ebola on the island could pose a far more dangerous risk and increase the odds of a rapid spread in the Western Hemisphere.

Cuba has a long tradition of dispatching doctors and nurses to disaster areas abroad. In the aftermath of Hurricane Katrina in 2005, the Cuban government created a quick-reaction medical corps and offered to send doctors to New Orleans. The United States, unsurprisingly, didn't take Havana up on that offer. Yet officials in Washington seemed thrilled to learn in recent weeks that Cuba had activated the medical teams for missions in Sierra Leone, Liberia and Guinea. . . .

In a column published over the weekend in Cuba's state-run newspaper, *Granma*, Fidel Castro argued that the United States and Cuba must put aside their differences, if only temporarily, to combat a deadly scourge. He's absolutely right.

Despite the editorial's intentions, the system couldn't understand Cuban medical cooperation as anything other than an act of self-interest. "Cuba's contribution is doubtlessly meant at least in part to bolster its beleaguered international standing," the editorial stated. To readers unfamiliar with the facts, this would seem normal. They would not be aware that Cuba—the Cuban Revolution—had extended medical solidarity to 109 countries between May 1960 and December 2014.

Such readers would not know that between 1970 and 2015, Cuba had provided assistance in disaster situations to the following countries: Peru (1970), Chile (1971), Nicaragua (1972, 1988, 1998, 2000–2003), Honduras (1974, 1998, 2000–2003), Algeria (1980, 2003), Mexico (1985), El Salvador (1986, 2000–2003), Ecuador (1987, 2000–2003), Armenia (1988), Iran (1990), the Dominican Republic (1998), Guatemala (1998), Haiti (1998), Colombia (1999), Venezuela (1999), Kosovo (1999), Sri Lanka (2005), Guyana (2005), and Indonesia (2006).

This included both countries with and countries without friendly governments—or sometimes even hostile governments, as in the case of Somoza's Nicaragua at the time of the 1972 earthquake.

Following Fidel's 2005 initiative to launch the Henry Reeve International Contingent of Medical Specialists in Disasters and Serious Epidemics, hundreds of Cuban health-care personnel had tackled natural or social emergencies in Guatemala, Pakistan, Indonesia, Bolivia, Peru, Belize, Mexico, China, El Salvador, Chile, Haiti, Sierra Leone, Liberia, Guinea and, as I write these lines, Chile and Nepal.[2]

It should be added that Cuba's collaboration—as the proverb goes—has not only brought fish to the hungry but has taught them how to fish. Cuba practices community and preventive medicine as well as primary, secondary, and tertiary health care in many countries. At the same time, it contributes to the creation of national health systems, builds and launches hospitals and medical schools, and offers scholarships to hundreds of young people from very poor countries. In the 2015–2016 school year, for example, some 10,000 medical students from other countries enrolled in Cuban universities. In addition, Cuba prepares and implements literacy programs adapted to different languages, even in countries of the so-called First World such as Spain.

Medical students in Cuba are trained to act as internationalists. According to a September 2015 statement from the health ministry published in *Granma International*, Cuba had "more than 85,000 doctors and the world's highest per capita rate: 7.7 doctors per 1,000 inhabitants, or one doctor for every 130 persons. Taking into account the 25,000 Cuban doctors on missions abroad, these num-

---

2. *Anuario*, issue 4 (2014), publication of Cuba's Central Medical Cooperation Unit.

bers yield a rate of 5.4 per 1,000, still among the highest worldwide." A veritable army of 46,500 young Cubans are currently studying medicine in our country's universities.

Traditional commentators, both of the right and the left, have difficulty understanding the character of Cuban solidarity. They have trouble placing it in the context of a Cuban tradition that for more than half a century has meant a foreign policy reflecting and developing a national model of a society based on solidarity, an heir in its essence to what is known as twentieth-century proletarian internationalism.

At the same time, Cuba's solidarity is different because of Fidel's political contributions and the unique circumstances of the country practicing it and of this historic period. In the case of Cuba, we're speaking not of a global power with geopolitical interests or extraterritorial economic aspirations, as could have been or can be the case with other states.

Cuba's solidarity has promoted mutual dependence among economies and societies that are poor, and this solidarity is viewed by its recipients not as a favor but as an irreplaceable ethical policy for those who practice it. Cuban internationalists don't "preach," but their conduct flows from a revolutionary outlook. You extend solidarity because you're a revolutionary—because solidarity is the foundation of a revolutionary society. You're not a revolutionary because you're a Marxist, but because you are one with the poor, the humble, the "fragile" of whom Pope Francis (who contributed to the restoration of US-Cuban diplomatic relations) spoke in Havana. Marxism is an expression of this course, and if at any time the theory or the ideas fail, or the world shifts, the priority remains advancing the interests of the poor, the humble, the fragile.

Because we have revolutionary power, everyone receives

medical care—both rich and poor, friend and enemy, communists and those with neoliberal ideas. You don't talk about political or ideological issues when you're saving a human life, although experience shows social problems can be solved when the political will exists. Cuban volunteers respect the traditions and laws of the countries where they work.

The medical bourgeoisie throughout Latin America knows that Cubans don't need to talk about politics—they're practicing their beliefs when they go to the most isolated places and save lives without asking for the patient's checkbook. The US policy that encourages Cuban health workers in other countries to defect—a policy that was condemned by the *New York Times*—continues despite the reestablishment of US-Cuba relations.

On September 3, 2015, Cuba's health ministry said the following in the press release cited above:

> The remarkable prestige our public health system enjoys around the world has led clinics in other countries to become interested in hiring Cuban professionals for private medical practice. This has even happened in friendly countries whose governments do not support or take part in such efforts.
>
> One of the main promoters of the brain drain has been the US government, which since the very first years of the revolution forced us to adopt measures and migratory regulations to counter this. The US government has continued its destabilization efforts though immigration lotteries, a policy of selective immigration, and the Cuban Adjustment Act.[3]

---

3. The 1966 Cuban Adjustment Act grants permanent residency to Cubans after one year in the US, a measure not applied to immigrants

The Cuban Medical Professional Parole Program, established in August 2006 during the George W. Bush administration, remains in force. It is designed to incite defection by Cuban medical professionals carrying out missions in other countries. The US government uses agents and activists, in areas where Cuban doctors are working under agreements with the host governments, to pressure and provide all kinds of resources to those who defect and emigrate to the United States. They promise them a better professional future, which in reality is possible only for a small minority.[4]

In recent years Cuba—economically blockaded and striving to survive in a world where, almost alone, it remains determined to build an alternative road for its people—has pursued compensation agreements with countries that can pay for its medical cooperation. That does not change the essence of what was described above.

In the case of very poor countries, such as Haiti or West African nations, Cuba does not ask them for compensation for its medical aid. In some cases a third country or an in-

---

from any other country. It encourages Cubans to try to enter the United States outside legal channels, often by risking a trip aboard flimsy rafts. In January 2017, in the final days of the Obama administration, the US government ended its two-decade-long "wet foot, dry foot" policy, which by guaranteeing US residency to any Cuban who set foot on US soil had led to numerous deaths in the Florida Straits. The Cuban Adjustment Act, however, remains in force.

4. The Cuban Medical Professional Parole Program was halted in the final week of the Obama administration; some US opponents of the Cuban Revolution have called for its reinstatement. Since then, however, Washington has stepped up its pressure on governments to no longer accept Cuban volunteer doctors. It has also denied visas to officials of the Cuba's health ministry, which oversees that country's international medical cooperation program.

"It's an elementary duty to aid Central America. We will send all the doctors necessary, for as long as needed. And we've offered a program to train Central Americans as doctors."

—Fidel Castro, November 1998, after Hurricane Mitch

PHOTOS BY ENRIQUE UBIETA GÓMEZ

After hurricane devastated Central America in 1998, the Cuban government sent 2,000 volunteer doctors and nurses. It began a program of Cuban medical brigades working in region. And it launched the Latin American School of Medicine, which has trained, free of charge, thousands of youth from those countries and others.

Top: Northern Guatemala, 1999. Two Cuban health-care workers (in back) with patients.

Bottom: Raití, Nicaragua, 1999. Mothers bring children to be vaccinated by Cuban doctors in Miskito indigenous community on Atlantic Coast.

Cuba's volunteer doctors serving around the world have long been a special target of Washington, which fears their example and what they demonstrate about Cuba's socialist revolution.

Ciriboya, Honduras, 2007. Opening of first hospital ever in region where most residents are Garífuna, a people of mixed African and indigenous descent. Hospital was founded by Garífuna graduates of Cuba's Latin American School of Medicine.

Tegucigalpa, Honduras, 2017. Cuban medical volunteers are welcomed at airport. Local medical guild has pressed government to expel Cuban doctors, who since 1998 have served in rural areas where most Honduran doctors refuse to work. Hundreds of residents have organized protests to block expulsion.

ternational entity such as the World Health Organization agrees to cover the cost of that aid.

Cuban doctors, nurses, and technicians working abroad are usually not based in large cities but in remote areas of the country. They receive fair compensation, similar in most cases to the concept of a stipend, and much less than what NGO employees from the First World are paid. But their relationships are with human beings, not with clients.

The Cuban people's support and admiration for those who fought the Ebola epidemic, and for the conduct of those who put their lives on the line, come from its sense of solidarity. Cuba's solidarity has nothing to do with the Manifest Destiny proclaimed by the US government—the assertion that it's bringing democracy to the rest of the world.

There were those who "explained" Cuba's decades-long solidarity in Africa before 1991—including the sending of guerrilla fighters, military missions, and medical, educational, and other civilian volunteers—by claiming it was part of a supposed international division of labor within the socialist system during the so-called Cold War, or that Cuba was politically subordinate to the Soviet Union. They are wrong.

How can those arguments explain the expansion of Cuba's medical and educational internationalism promoted by Fidel after Hurricane Mitch hit Central America in 1998—in the midst of the century's greatest battle of ideas, when part of the left was jumping ship and scrambling to reach the shore?

Those who, in an atmosphere of disillusionment and cynical doubts, claim that Cuba's solidarity today is simply a move on an international geopolitical chessboard, or a commercially motivated survival maneuver, are obscuring the facts. The solid arguments and documentation presented in Piero Gleijeses's book *Conflicting Missions* help us understand this history, which also offers the best path to understand the present.

I believe it would have been useful if a left-wing author like Adame Cerón had raised a few questions regarding epidemics and so-called humanitarian interventions in his interesting analysis of imperialist policies in the new century, given the significant role that Cuba plays in these important events:

- Beyond the official discourse, is Cuba really welcomed by those who monopolize, distribute, organize, and make decisions on transnational "solidarity"?

- To what extent does Cuba's solidarity offer examples that are counterposed to the "solidarity" of military interventions and even to the lucrative efforts of certain NGOs that defend hegemonic interests?

- Is Cuba correct or not in offering to cooperate in health care with governments that don't represent the interests of their people, or with international capitalist institutions—even the Atlanta CDC or the US Army—when this leads to person-to-person relations in the country where the solidarity is offered and results in lives saved? Above all, is this revolutionary or not?

- Why do enemies of the Cuban Revolution so viciously attack and try to discredit this solidarity? Why have they created policies that encourage Cuban internationalists to defect?

- Finally, to what extent does internationalism help foster socialist values in Cuban society?

Of course, Adame could argue that this would be another book. His explanations, however, don't answer a question I consider essential: What is Cuba doing there? What role does it play?

I don't believe Cuba's presence in the fight against Ebola

led to the reestablishment of diplomatic relations with the United States. I don't think the United States, its imperialist system, now accepts coexistence with a socialist state close to its shores. It's simply a change in its interventionist methods.

The reasons for this change are not Cuba's "good behavior," much less its medical internationalism, but rather recognition by the US establishment that the methods of direct confrontation used so far have not only been ineffectual and counterproductive, but detrimental to the increasingly declining US leadership position in the hemisphere. And because they believe the time has come for a person-to-person approach, of a new and (they hope) deadly version of the "Good Neighbor" policy after five decades of warlike tensions. US politicians have said as much.

In any case, Obama's decision, even from his own perspective, was courageous. The secret talks between the two governments began long before Cuba sent volunteers to the countries ravaged by the epidemic. But the media coverage of Cuba's cooperation in West Africa—and this does seem important to me—helped create a favorable context for making such a decision.

On December 17, 2014, the presidents of Cuba and the United States made simultaneous announcements of their decision to reestablish diplomatic relations. The US government had broken relations with Cuba's revolutionary government in 1961, and it restored them with the same revolutionary government. It broke relations with Fidel's revolution, and restored them with Fidel's revolution.

In his historic speech, President Obama referred to the possibility of cooperation with Cuba around humanitarian aid, something Fidel had always suggested. Obama said:

Where we can advance shared interests, we will—on issues like health, migration, counterterrorism, drug trafficking, and disaster response. . . .

Cuba has sent hundreds of health care workers to Africa to fight Ebola, and I believe American and Cuban health care workers should work side by side to stop the spread of this deadly disease.

The Ebola Treatment Unit where doctors and nurses of the Henry Reeve Contingent worked in Liberia was donated by the United States, but Cuban medical personnel worked with those from the US in its design and proposed modifications in the project that were taken into account. On the ground, where real people came face to face, yes, there was real collaboration. The person in charge of Phase 3 training for the Cubans in Liberia was a young microbiologist from the Atlanta CDC, an Ebola specialist.

Nonetheless, the first photos taken by the volunteers, which appeared in the Cuban press, showed the extent to which US government agencies publicized their own aid. The field hospital had "USAID" printed all over its tarp—an acronym that is far from friendly in the history of US-Latin American relations, including in Cuba, of course. The US Agency for International Development (USAID) has for decades served as a cover for the CIA's subversive financial operations.

Yet when the US ambassador, accompanying the Liberian president, inaugurated the new Ebola Treatment Unit, she twice referred to the doctors and nurses of the Henry Reeve Contingent. And she used a phrase in Spanish that surprised them, to say the least: "I extend a greeting to my Cuban friends."

In Sierra Leone, too, a "clash" between the actual human beings involved ended up demolishing myths and prejudices. Dr. Luis Escalona Gutiérrez, deputy head of the Cuban brigade there, told me:

> We were working in Maforki–Port Loko with Partners in Health, a US nongovernmental organization based in Boston. At first they kept some distance from us; they had prejudices. But from the very first week they began to understand we were there to work and they opened up. Solid ties were established, to the point that they put up our flags in their living quarters and we put up their flags in ours.
>
> Since they had some financial resources, they gave us a refrigerator and fans for use in the treatment unit. They sometimes also provided us with water, a vital necessity in short supply in these units. You know how dehydrated you get every time you go in. The US doctors and nurses would wait for us so we could enter the red zone together. There was a certain rapport. They admired the professionalism and courage of our team.
>
> At first they wouldn't touch the patients. But when they saw that the Cubans touched and washed the patients and inserted IV lines, they said, "Well, if you do it, why not us?"
>
> Unfortunately, after our departure a Partners in Health doctor came down with Ebola, but his life was saved. Partners in Health physicians were very ethical and dedicated to their profession; the big majority stayed away from politics. The December 17 announcement drew brief comments from them: "Very good," "It's about time."

In fact, Partners in Health had already worked with Cubans in Haiti. The group's executive director, Dr. Paul Farmer, enjoyed excellent relations with the Cuban medical directors.

But despite the diplomatic talks and official statements,

New York Times editorials, demands of the international community, and even common sense, the US blockade continued to be felt as if nothing had changed, at least in Sierra Leone. Dr. Jorge Delgado Bustillo, head of the Cuban mission there, told me:

> We've had to fight to overcome many obstacles, including financial ones. We were blocked by the US Treasury Department's OFAC [Office of Foreign Assets Control]. We spent the entire month of November and part of December without receiving a penny, unable to pay for hotels or give volunteers their stipends. The Cuban mission couldn't open a bank account, as Geneva assumed we had. They thought we would open an account in my name, but we said no, the account should be in the name of the Cuban medical mission, with three well-known signatories. So obstacles arose.
>
> We had to resort to a strategy in which WHO would pay the hotels directly by bank transfer in the local currency. I mean, in what country of the world would you have a situation with 100 non-paying guests? . . .
>
> I have to admit, though, that despite the pressure from the owners of the Barmoy and the Seaside hotels, who called me every day from the United States, where they lived, they were patient and waited for the problems to be resolved. It wasn't straightened out in October, or in November. In late October we received two payments that allowed us to give something to our colleagues so they could start charging their cell phones and computers and contact their relatives. Everything began to be resolved by mid-December.
>
> Because of OFAC regulations, we faced restrictions not only on the bank account but on how much we could withdraw each week.

> We've complied rigorously with our obligations to WHO. Every penny received has been duly audited by WHO. We have a good accountant, but we all act in that capacity. Even the deputy head of the brigade, Dr. Escalona, took part in the accounting, because four eyes are better than two. We're leaving April 1. On Monday, March 30, at the latest, we'll hand over everything.

Dr. Luis Escalona smiles and recalls those uncertain days:

> That initial month and a half was the most critical period, because we were about to be evicted from the hotel. We even came up with a drastic solution, but after we sat down to discuss things we realized we had to see it through, no matter what.

The deputy head of the US diplomatic mission attended the December 19, 2014, inauguration of the Ebola Treatment Unit in Coyah, Guinea, knowing the new center would be led by Cubans and Africans. It was two days after the announcement on the reestablishment of diplomatic relations between the two historic enemies. The US ambassador to Guinea himself visited the center twice and, along with other members of his delegation, chatted with the Cuban volunteers in Spanish.

The governments of the three countries felt pleased that the first apparent understanding between the United States and Cuba took place on African territory. It was in Africa where, over the decades, the blood shed and solidarity extended by Cubans had forged a relationship with African peoples that went beyond any ideological or geopolitical explanations.

Africa was also where some of the sharpest clashes with

242 DAVID, GOLIATH, AND OTHER REFLECTIONS

imperialism had taken place. Combatants from this small Caribbean island battled alongside fighters from Algeria, the Congo, Guinea-Bissau, Angola, and Namibia for their respective countries' independence, and backed liberation movements across the continent.

Meanwhile, successive US administrations, locked into the narrow framework of the Cold War and their international doctrine of "national security," acted directly or indirectly in support of local allies who were alien or opposed to African interests.

Foreign minister Augustine Kpehe Ngafuan of Liberia, a country with historic ties to the United States, said with obvious enthusiasm:

> In Liberia we have Cuban doctors helping us at the Ebola Treatment Unit in facilities that belonged to the Ministry of Defense. In Liberia we have American doctors helping us. In Liberia you came together, and it did not take long to learn the wonderful news. We can therefore say that Liberian soil offers the basis for cooperation at a higher level.
>
> I think President Obama can point to the fact that cooperation in the field of health is flourishing. So we strongly support the new developments in relations between Cuba and the United States of America, and we wish you the best.
>
> We have close bilateral relations with the United States and we have close bilateral relations with Cuba. You are both great friends of ours, and we hope our great friends shall also become great friends.
>
> Liberia is a member of several continental political and economic organizations. We are part of the Economic Community of West African States (ECOWAS) and belong to the African Union, where there is a strong position in favor of rejecting the "blockade." We also support

that position bilaterally and consistently vote that way. We hope this will not have to be put to a vote once again.

Dr. Samura Kamara, Sierra Leone's foreign minister, said:

> I think the beginning of friendly discussions between Cuba and the United States is a positive development in international politics. We are pleased by the building of a cordial relationship between Cuba and the United States. We hope for a quick solution in this regard.

Guinean foreign minister Lounceny Fall also spoke about this historic event when we asked him why his government has consistently supported Cuba in the United Nations vote against the blockade:

> It's only natural. We have not only supported but co-sponsored the General Assembly resolution along with many other African countries. The reason is simple. We consider the embargo unjust and we must do justice for the Cuban people. The embargo that Cuba has been suffering under for years must be lifted.
>
> That's why at the last African Union (AU) summit meeting we and other countries requested the AU adopt a resolution, above all, to salute and encourage President Obama and President Raúl [for announcing that the process of reestablishing relations had begun] and to urge President Obama to use all his powers to get Congress to rapidly lift the embargo.
>
> In speaking to Africans, we argue that no country in the world has helped Africa lift itself up as much as Cuba has. Cuba has helped Africa, its liberation movements, and we cannot abandon Cuba in face of hard-

ships. A natural solidarity has developed between Cuba and Africa. As long as the embargo is maintained, we will continue to insist the United States lift it. Besides, consider the fact that more than one hundred countries vote against the embargo at the UN. The US president has said that when something doesn't work, it's time to change it.

The Cuban people have resisted heroically. I've been to Cuba several times. I think this embargo must be lifted. We hope the reestablishing of relations happens quickly and is followed by the lifting of the embargo. That will bring peace to that part of the world and provide justice for the Cuban people.

President Alpha Condé of Guinea talked about this in his exchange with our press team. He gave us some insights:

When the Cuban doctors arrived the US ambassador told me, "It's you who got the Cubans and Americans to talk to each other today." That was before Obama decided to reestablish relations.

So we want to strengthen our relations with Cuba. Above all, I want to travel to Cuba while Fidel is still alive. It's not just to visit Cuba but to pay tribute to President Fidel Castro for all the support he has given—to Guinea and to all liberation struggles in Africa. We've always opposed the blockade against Cuba and we've always called for lifting it at UN meetings.

On July 28, 2015, during an African Union meeting in Addis Ababa to which US president Barack Obama was invited, a joint statement was issued. A news dispatch reported:

In a historic and moving speech, Dr. Nkosazana Dlamini Zuma, chairperson of the African Union Commission, speaking on behalf of all African countries, thanked President Obama, who listened attentively, for the decision to reestablish diplomatic relations with Cuba. She described it as an act of historic justice for the Cuban people.

Chairperson Zuma's exact words were: "Africa remains seized with the issues facing Diaspora everywhere, and we therefore applaud your leadership towards the normalization of relations between the USA and Cuba. It seemed impossible when, in 1973, President Fidel Castro in an interview predicted that a resolution shall be found when the US has itself its first black president, and the world has a Latin American Pope. We wish you, honorable president and the Cubans, all the best in these endeavors."

When the event concluded, the entire plenary stood up and applauded, chanting "Long live Cuba" and "Long live Fidel."[5]

---

5. *Tralac*, publication of Trade Law Centre in Western Cape, South Africa, July 28, 2015.

AFTERWORD

We attended the tribute the Liberian government held for the Cuban doctors and nurses a few days before their departure. Then we accompanied the first group from the Sierra Leone brigade to the airport as they returned home. Some were carrying big stuffed animals for their small children back in Cuba—as small as the kids they had saved or lost, as those who had been orphaned, in the battle against Ebola.

Also traveling on the plane were the members of the Liberia brigade, since Monrovia had been the first stop on the flight. We said good-bye to the men at the foot of the boarding stairs, and then even sneaked up the steps to greet those already aboard.

We weren't able to say goodbye to the Guinea brigade at that time. At the request of the Guinean president, after negotiations with WHO, some members of that brigade agreed to stay an extra month. Others returned at the end of the initial agreed-on period, for various reasons that were accepted. But it was inspiring to learn that most said they were willing to remain as long as necessary.

Once back in Cuba, we all went through the quarantine period, myself included. Almost all the doctors and nurses did so at a specially equipped school in Jagüey Grande, Matanzas province. In a sad twist of fate, two additional Cuban brigade members died after they had returned and resumed their life in Cuba. The first, Jesús Pérez Sosa, died of a heart attack. Jacinto Ortuzar Mauri died of an illness that developed suddenly.

On July 9, 2015, Cuba's Council of State awarded the Carlos J. Finlay Order to 248 brigade members. The four who had died, two in Africa and two in Cuba, were posthumously decorated. Ambassadors Maité Rivero Torres and Jorge Lefebre, as well as the chargés d'affaires in Liberia and Sierra Leone, Pedro Luis Despaigne and Antonio Pubillones, received the Extraordinary Labor Achievement medal. The awards were presented by José Ramón Machado Ventura, second secretary of the Communist Party of Cuba's Central Committee and a vice president of the Councils of State and Ministers.

A letter from President Raúl Castro was read, in which he noted:

> Having carried out the honorable mission that took you to West Africa six months ago—even at the risk of your own lives—to combat the Ebola outbreak devastating the continent, you returned to the homeland, which welcomed you back with utmost pride.
>
> On behalf of the Cuban people as well as myself, I bestow this recognition on you for the heroic work you undertook as part of the Henry Reeve International Contingent.
>
> You represent a continuation of the altruism and selflessness that has marked our country's medical cooperation since 1963 with the sending of the first brigade to Algeria under the leadership of the minister of public health at that time, compañero José Ramón Machado Ventura. Over these years, 158 countries have benefited from the solidarity of 325,710 Cuban volunteers.

The experience in Africa was unique. We got to know extraordinary, unassuming Cubans. Many had carried out previous missions in Asia, Africa, or Latin America. Some had participated in the wars in Angola or Nicaragua. Others had worked in communities devastated by major epidemics or natural disasters. All had come to know the extreme poverty and inequality of the world that we share. I also met Cubans on their first hazardous mission—some very young. They were no less courageous or competent. For some, the epic spirit is part of a past that cannot be recaptured. Cuba today is a more diverse and spiritually rich society, thanks to the revolution, and many people seem to be consumed with their individual affairs. The US blockade continues, and it punishes average Cubans. But whenever there is a call to action, thousands of volunteers step forward.

Fidel is in a league of his own, but that doesn't mean we should limit our dreams. Those who believe that without him we cannot meet the great challenges we face have no confidence in the people and their heroic history, nor do they understand Fidel. That's what the imperialists think, which is why we can defeat them. The hundreds of doctors and nurses who volunteered and those who went to West Africa are irrefutable proof of a fact: among the people there are moral reserves—reserves that need to be summoned.

REFERENCES CITED IN THIS BOOK

Adame Cerón, Miguel Ángel, *Ébola y la mundialización epidémica* (Ebola and epidemic globalization; Mexico City: Ediciones Navarra, 2014).

Gleijeses, Piero, *Conflicting Missions: Havana, Washington, and Africa, 1959-1976* (Chapel Hill: University of North Carolina Press, 2002).

González López, David, y Pulido Escandell, Clara: "Viejos y nuevos conflictos en la ecuación etnia-Estado-sociedad en el África Subsahariana" (Old and new conflicts in the ethnic-state-society equation in sub-Saharan Africa), *Cuadernos África-América Latina*, no. 27-28, 1997. Journal published by SODePAZ, Madrid.

Niang, Cheikh Ibrahima, "Ebola diaries: Lessons in listening," May 2015, World Health Organization, www.who.int/features/2015/ebola-diaries-niang/en

Preston, Richard, *The Hot Zone* (New York: Random House, 1994).

Pulido Escandell, Clara, "La mediación regional en los conflictos africanos: el caso de ECOMOG en Liberia" (Regional mediation in African conflicts: the case of ECOMOG in Liberia), *Revista de África y Medio Oriente*, no. 1, 1996. Journal published by the Center for African and Middle Eastern Studies, Havana.

Stavenhagen, Rodolfo, *Ethnic Conflicts and the Nation-State* (London: McMillan, 1996).

Ubieta Gómez, Enrique, *La utopía rearmada: Historias de un viaje al nuevo mundo* (Utopia rearmed: Report on a trip to the New World; Havana: Casa Editora Abril, 2002).

INDEX

Note: The name of an individual followed by a country in parentheses—for example, "Abeleira, René (Sierra Leone)"—indicates a Cuban medical volunteer and country served in.

The Cuban Revolution ...

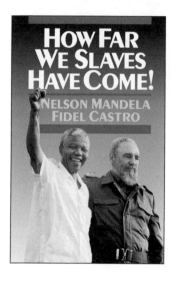

How Far We Slaves Have Come!

South Africa and Cuba
in Today's World

NELSON MANDELA, FIDEL CASTRO

Speaking together in Cuba in 1991,
Mandela and Castro discuss the role
of Cuba in the history of Africa and
Angola's victory over the invading
US-backed South African army. That
victory accelerated the fight to bring
down the racist apartheid system. $7.
Also in Spanish and Farsi.

Cuba and Angola
The War for Freedom

HARRY VILLEGAS ("POMBO")

 &

Cuba and Angola

Fighting for Africa's Freedom and Our Own

FIDEL CASTRO, RAÚL CASTRO,
NELSON MANDELA

Two books that tell the story of Cuba's
unparalleled contribution to the fight to free
Africa from the scourge of apartheid. And how,
in the doing, Cuba's socialist revolution was also
strengthened. $10 and $12. Also in Spanish.

From the Escambray to the Congo

In the Whirlwind of the Cuban Revolution

VÍCTOR DREKE

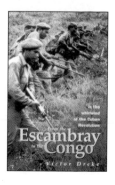

Dreke was second in command of the internationalist
column in the Congo led in 1965 by Che Guevara. He
recounts the creative joy with which working people
have defended their revolutionary course—from
Cuba's Escambray mountains to Africa and beyond.
$15. Also in Spanish.

... *its impact from Africa to US*

The Bolivian Diary of Ernesto Che Guevara

Guevara's day-by-day chronicle of the 1966–67 guerrilla campaign in Bolivia, an effort to forge a continent-wide revolutionary movement of workers and peasants and open the road to socialist revolution in South America. $23. Also in Spanish.

Cuba and the Coming American Revolution

JACK BARNES

This is a book about the struggles of working people in the imperialist heartland, the youth attracted to them, and the example set by the Cuban people that revolution is not only necessary—it can be made. It is about the class struggle in the US, where the revolutionary capacities of workers and farmers are today as utterly discounted by the ruling powers as were those of the Cuban toilers. And just as wrongly. $10. Also in Spanish, French, and Farsi.

Che Guevara: Economics and Politics in the Transition to Socialism

CARLOS TABLADA

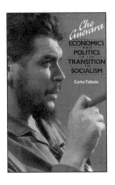

Quoting extensively from Guevara's writings and speeches on building socialism, this book presents the interrelationship of the market, economic planning, material incentives, and voluntary work. Guevara shows why profit and other capitalist categories cannot be yardsticks for progress in the transition to socialism. $17. Also in Spanish, French, and Greek.

Capitalism and the Transformation of Africa

Reports from Equatorial Guinea

MARY-ALICE WATERS, MARTÍN KOPPEL

Describes how, as Equatorial Guinea is pulled into the world market, both a capitalist class and a working class are being born. Also documents the work of volunteer Cuban health-care workers there—an expression of the living example of Cuba's socialist revolution. $10. Also in Spanish and Farsi.

FROM PATHFINDER

The Turn to Industry: Forging a Proletarian Party

JACK BARNES

A book about the working-class program, composition, and course of conduct of the only kind of party worthy of the name "revolutionary" in the imperialist epoch. A party that can recognize the most revolutionary fact of this epoch—the worth of working people, and our power to change society when we organize and act against the capitalist class in all its economic, social, and political forms. It's about building such a party in the US and in other capitalist countries around the world. $15. Also in Spanish.

Tribunes of the People and the Trade Unions

KARL MARX, V.I. LENIN, LEON TROTSKY, FARRELL DOBBS, JACK BARNES

A tribune of the people uses every example of capitalist oppression to explain why working people, in class battles, will lay the foundations of a socialist world of human solidarity. $12. Also in Spanish.

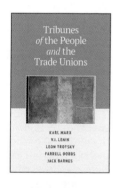

The Clintons' Anti-Working-Class Record

Why Washington Fears Working People

JACK BARNES

What working people need to know about the profit-driven course of Democrats and Republicans alike over the last thirty years. And the political awakening of workers seeking to understand and resist the capitalist rulers' assaults. $10. Also in Spanish, French, Farsi, and Greek.

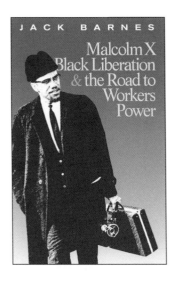

Malcolm X, Black Liberation, and the Road to Workers Power

JACK BARNES

The conquest of state power by a class-conscious vanguard of the working class is the mightiest weapon working people can wield against racism and Black oppression, as well as every form of human degradation inherited from class society. $20. Also in Spanish, French, Farsi, Arabic, and Greek.

Are They Rich Because They're Smart?

Class, Privilege, and Learning under Capitalism

JACK BARNES

An answer to middle class layers who see working people of all colors as "deplorables" or just "trash." Who think their own "brightness" equips them to "regulate" the rest of us. $10. Also in Spanish, French, and Farsi.

Is Socialist Revolution in the US Possible?

A Necessary Debate among Working People

MARY-ALICE WATERS

Fighting for a society only working people can create, it is our own capacities we will discover. And along that course we will answer the question posed here with a resounding "Yes." Possible but not inevitable. That depends on us. $7. Also in Spanish, French, and Farsi.

In Defense of the US Working Class

MARY-ALICE WATERS

Drawing on the best fighting traditions of workers of all skin colors and national origin in 2018, tens of thousands of working people in states like West Virginia, Oklahoma, and Florida waged victorious strikes and won restoration of voting rights to former prisoners. Those who Hillary Clinton calls "deplorables" have begun to fight back. $7. Also in Spanish, French, and Farsi.

The Long View of History

GEORGE NOVACK

Why and how the revolutionary struggle by working people to end millennia of oppression and exploitation is a realistic perspective. $5. Also in Farsi.

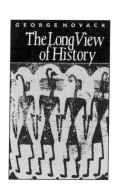

The Communist Manifesto

KARL MARX AND FREDERICK ENGELS

Communism, say the founding leaders of the revolutionary workers movement, is not a preconceived doctrine but workers' line of march to power, springing from "an existing class struggle, from a historical movement going on under our very eyes." $5. Also in Spanish, French, Farsi, and Arabic.

ALSO FROM PATHFINDER

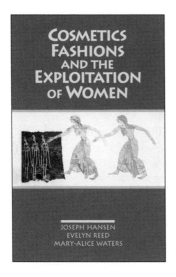

Cosmetics, Fashions, and the Exploitation of Women

JOSEPH HANSEN, EVELYN REED, MARY-ALICE WATERS

How big business plays on women's second-class status in class society and what Reed calls "capitalist social compulsion" to market cosmetics and rake in profits. And how the entry of millions of women into the workforce has irreversibly changed relations between women and men—for the better. $12. Also in Spanish and Farsi.

Puerto Rico: Independence Is a Necessity

RAFAEL CANCEL MIRANDA

One of the five Puerto Rican Nationalists imprisoned by Washington for more than 25 years and released in 1979 speaks out on the brutal reality of US colonial domination, the example of Cuba's socialist revolution, and the ongoing struggle for independence. $5. Also in Spanish and Farsi.

Art and Revolution

Writings on Literature, Politics, and Culture

LEON TROTSKY

"Art can become a strong ally of revolution only insofar as it remains faithful to itself," wrote Trotsky in 1938. $15

"It's the Poor Who Face the Savagery of the US 'Justice' System"

The Cuban Five Talk about Their Lives within the US Working Class

How US cops, courts, and prisons work as "an enormous machine for grinding people up." Five Cuban revolutionaries framed up and held in US jails for 16 years explain the human devastation of capitalist "justice"—and how socialist Cuba is different. $10. Also in Spanish, Farsi, and Greek.

REVOLUTIONARY LEADERS IN THEIR OWN WORDS

Malcolm X Talks to Young People

"The young generation of whites, Blacks, browns, whatever else there is— you're living at a time of revolution," Malcolm said in December 1964. "And I for one will join in with anyone, I don't care what color you are, as long as you want to change this miserable condition that exists on this earth." $12. Also in Spanish, French, Farsi, and Greek.

The Transitional Program for Socialist Revolution

LEON TROTSKY

The Socialist Workers Party program, drafted by Trotsky in 1938, still guides the SWP and communists the world over. The party "uncompromisingly gives battle to all political groupings tied to the apron strings of the bourgeoisie. Its task—the abolition of capitalism's domination. Its aim—socialism. Its method—the proletarian revolution." $17. Also in Farsi.

Maurice Bishop Speaks

The Grenada Revolution and Its Overthrow, 1979–83

The triumph of the 1979 revolution in the Caribbean island of Grenada under the leadership of Maurice Bishop gave hope to millions throughout the Americas. Invaluable lessons from the workers and farmers government destroyed by a Stalinist-led counterrevolution in 1983. $20

The Teamster series

FARRELL DOBBS

From the 1934 strikes that won union recognition to the fight by class-conscious workers to oppose Washington's objectives in World War II.

"These books are not 'manuals' or handbooks. They are the record of a concrete experience in the class struggle—one that can be studied and absorbed by class-conscious workers and farmers who find themselves in the midst of other struggles, at other times, in other conditions, speaking many different languages."—Jack Barnes. $16 each. Also in Spanish. *Teamster Rebellion* is available in French, Farsi, and Greek.

Revolutionary Continuity

Marxist Leadership in the United States
The Early Years, 1848–1917
Birth of the Communist Movement, 1918–1922

FARRELL DOBBS

Two volumes, $17 each.

"Successive generations of proletarian revolutionists have participated in the movements of the working class and its allies. . . . Marxists today owe them not only homage for their deeds. We also have a duty to learn what they did wrong as well as right so their errors are not repeated."—Farrell Dobbs

Lenin's Final Fight

Speeches and Writings, 1922–23

V.I. LENIN

In 1922 and 1923, V.I. Lenin, central leader of the world's first socialist revolution, waged what was to be his last political battle—one that was lost following his death. At stake was whether that revolution, and the international communist movement it led, would remain on the revolutionary proletarian course that brought workers and peasants to power in October 1917. $17. Also in Spanish, Farsi, and Greek.

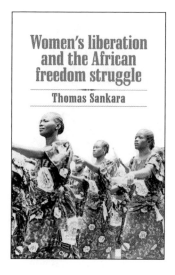

Women's Liberation and the African Freedom Struggle

THOMAS SANKARA

"There is no true social revolution without the liberation of women," explains the leader of the 1983–87 revolution in the West African country of Burkina Faso. $5. Also in Spanish, French, and Farsi.

Socialism on Trial

Testimony at Minneapolis Sedition Trial

JAMES P. CANNON

The revolutionary program of the working class, presented in response to frame-up charges of "seditious conspiracy" in 1941, on the eve of US entry into World War II. The defendants were leaders of the Minneapolis labor movement and the Socialist Workers Party. $15. Also in Spanish, French, and Farsi.

Women in Cuba: The Making of a Revolution Within the Revolution

VILMA ESPÍN, ASELA DE LOS SANTOS, YOLANDA FERRER

The integration of women into the ranks and leadership of the Cuban Revolution was inseparably intertwined with the proletarian course of the revolution from the start. This is the story of that revolution and how it transformed the women and men who made it. $17. Also in Spanish and Greek.

New International

A MAGAZINE OF MARXIST POLITICS AND THEORY

Capitalism's Long Hot Winter Has Begun

JACK BARNES

Today's global capitalist crisis is but the opening stage of decades of economic, financial, and social convulsions and class battles. Class-conscious workers confront this historic turning point for imperialism with confidence, Jack Barnes writes, drawing satisfaction from being "in their face" as we chart a revolutionary course to take power. In *New International* no. 12. $14. Also in Spanish, French, Farsi, Arabic, and Greek.

In Defense of Land and Labor

"Capitalist production only develops by simultaneously undermining the original sources of all wealth—the soil and the worker." —*Karl Marx, 1867.*

FOUR ARTICLES

IN *NEW INTERNATIONAL* NO. 13
- **Our Politics Start with the World**
  JACK BARNES
- **Farming, Science, and the Working Classes**
  STEVE CLARK
- **Capitalism, Labor, and the Transformation of Nature: An Exchange**
  RICHARD LEVINS, STEVE CLARK

IN *NEW INTERNATIONAL* NO. 14
- **The Stewardship of Nature Also Falls to the Working Class**
  JACK BARNES, STEVE CLARK, MARY-ALICE WATERS

$14 each issue

WWW.PATHFINDERPRESS.COM

PATHFINDER AROUND THE WORLD

Visit our website for a complete list of titles and to place orders

www.pathfinderpress.com

PATHFINDER DISTRIBUTORS

UNITED STATES
(and Caribbean, Latin America, and East Asia)

Pathfinder Books, 306 W. 37th St., 13th Floor
New York, NY 10018

CANADA

Pathfinder Books, 7107 St. Denis, Suite 204
Montreal, QC H2S 2S5

UNITED KINGDOM
(and Europe, Africa, Middle East, and South Asia)

Pathfinder Books, 5 Norman Rd.
Seven Sisters, London N15 4ND

AUSTRALIA
(and Southeast Asia and the Pacific)

Pathfinder Books, Suite 22, 10 Bridge St.
Granville, Sydney, NSW 2142

NEW ZEALAND

Pathfinder Books, 188a Onehunga Mall Rd., Onehunga, Auckland 1061
Postal address: P.O. Box 13857, Auckland 1643

Join the Pathfinder Readers Club
to get 25% discounts on all Pathfinder
titles and bigger discounts
on special offers.
Sign up at www.pathfinderpress.com
or through the distributors above.
$10 a year